Arthur Ransome

Twayne's English Authors Series
Children's Literature

Lois R. Kuznets, Editor
San Diego State University

TEAS 484

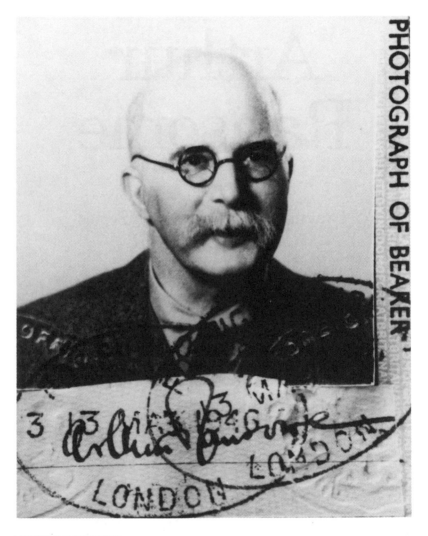

ARTHUR RANSOME
Passport photograph, reproduced courtesy of John Bell. Re–photographed by Nick Hackett.

Arthur Ransome

Peter Hunt

University of Wales, Cardiff

Twayne Publishers • Boston
A Division of G. K. Hall & Co.

Arthur Ransome
Peter Hunt

Copyright 1991 by G. K. Hall & Co.
All rights reserved.
Published by Twayne Publishers
A division of G. K. Hall & Co.
70 Lincoln Street
Boston, Massachusetts 02111

Copyediting supervised by Barbara Sutton.
Book production by Gabrielle B. McDonald.
Book design by Janet Z. Reynolds.
Typeset in Century Schoolbook by Compset, Inc., of Beverly, Massachusetts.

10 9 8 7 6 5 4 3 2 1

Printed and bound in the United States of America.

Library of Congress Cataloging-in-Publication Data

Hunt, Peter, 1945–
    Arthur Ransome / Peter Hunt.
        p.   cm. — (Twayne's English authors series ; v. TEAS 484)
    Includes bibliographical references and index.
    ISBN 0-8057-7003-8
    1. Ransome, Arthur, 1884–1967—Criticism and interpretation.
    2. Children's stories, English—History and criticism.   I. Title.
    II. Series.
    PR6035.A63Z65   1991
    823'.912—dc20   90-24572
                                                                     CIP

Contents

Illustrations

Preface

Roger, aged seven, and no longer the youngest of the family, ran in wide zigzags, to and fro, across the steep field that sloped up from the lake to Holly Howe, the farm where they were staying for part of the summer holidays.[1]

So begins *Swallows and Amazons,* the first of a series of twelve books that changed British children's literature, affected a whole generation's view of vacations, helped to create the national image of the English Lake District, and added Arthur Ransome's name to the select list of British "classic" children's book authors.

Almost every version of British children's-book history sees Ransome as a landmark figure. One critic has said his work "may well be used to mark the terminus of the Edwardian age".[2] According to another, "[his] contribution to the twentieth-century children's story was incalculable. He led the way to a more natural approach; to a realistic and unsentimental characterisation; to a completely true to life dialogue, and to a new conception of the kind of excitement necessary to keep children reading for pleasure."[3] Another writes that Ransome "killed laziness in the writing of children's stories".[4] He was awarded one of Britain's highest civil honors, the CBE (Commander of the Order of the British Empire), and an honorary doctorate—an exceptional thing for a writer of children's books. He raised the status of the profession of writing for children, and his influence is still with us.

Ransome's series, published between 1930 and 1948 (1931 and 1948 in the United States), takes just over a million words to describe the holiday adventures of three groups of children and their friends over four fictional years. The children "mess about in boats," sail, fish, and camp in the Lake District in the northwest of England and on the Norfolk Broads and in the estuaries of the east coast of England. In one book, four of them cross the North Sea to Holland in a small yacht (Ransome let his own yacht drift out to sea to check the authenticity of his plot). Three of the novels are "yarns," tales told to pass the winter evenings; they differ from the others in that, although they feature apparently the same "realistic" characters, the adventures are improbable and extravagant.

A key feature of the books is that most of them are based very solidly in reality. An early reviewer of *Swallows and Amazons* wrote: "One of the great charms of this book is its extreme reasonableness. Mr. Ransome is as thoughtful of detail as Defoe."[5] Ransome would have appreciated the comparison, for not only had he written about Defoe, he shared his democratic cast of mind, his utilitarianism and pragmatism.

The children, although perhaps a little too good-natured and lacking in traumas for today's tastes, are "real"; and they live in a recognizable world, with recognizable laws and values. With few exceptions, Ransome does not use the stock-in-trade of the children's adventure stories of his day. There are no "villains," no easy achievements, and no gratuitous triumphs over an "inferior" adult world. Everything is proportional to the children's abilities; the only thing at which children are better than adults is being children. Similarly, if his children are "free," it is a recognizable freedom; it implies and requires mutual responsibility and mutual respect. As a result, the children never lose their family or cultural identities.

But for all this unfashionable reference to codes of behavior, the books are exciting, and, it seems, eternally fascinating. They have become part of British culture, along with *Winnie-the-Pooh, Alice in Wonderland,* and *The Wind in the Willows,* and familiarity with them places one in an exclusive club—the kind of club where "we" are superior to outsiders.

In placing sailing at the center of the books, Ransome speaks to a whole culture and taps into a very potent group of associations. We may not be familiar with the world of transoms and cleats and sculling, but the narrator greets us as if we were, and, usually, lets us into the secrets. And because it is obvious that we are in a world of experts, that world is believable and *reliable,* a characteristic that short-circuits many of the usual problems, such as differences in class, race, or gender, that readers have in joining the world of a novel.

When Ransome wrote *Swallows and Amazons,* British children's books were passing through a drab age, sometimes described as an age of "brass" between two "golden" ages (one spanning the era 1870–1920, the other the 1950s and 1960s). There were strong divisions between books for boys and books for girls, and a massive output of second-rate "rewards" (books printed on cheap paper and intended as gifts).

The "Swallows and Amazons" series changed this trend in both dramatic and subtle ways. Most dramatically, Ransome involved his "ordinary" children in what he called "straightforward, possible events, in a world outside the door."[6] The family is still at the center of the children's world picture, but it is no longer depicted in the context of a house, nursery, or secret garden. The canvas is larger. The children fend for themselves in a world where adults, although around, are essentially peripheral beings—just as they are to real children. Yet the adult world is not in conflict with the children's world; each treats the other with respect.

Another strength is that Ransome used genuine landscapes. When he won the first British Library Association Carnegie Medal in 1936 (for the sixth book in the series, *Pigeon Post*), he commented:

> If you know a bit of country really well, it takes a very active part in the making of your book. You can count on it. It is always there and, somehow or other, life flows from it into your story. . . . In the case of the first book, I steered clear of using real names . . . so the Swallows and Amazons had a country of their own. . . . Then, too, there had to be a little pulling about of rivers and roads, but every single place in all those books exists somewhere and, by now, I know the geography of the country in the books so well that when I walk about in actual fact, it sometimes seems to me that some giant or earthquake has been doing a little scene-shifting overnight.[7]

The scant distinction Ransome makes between boys and girls in terms of skills and achievements is also significant. He is guilty of some sex-stereotyping, but by and large his boys and girls have equal, if distinctive, roles. If we add to these an implicit acceptance of decent behavior and practical moral codes, a stress on the real being as interesting as the fantastic, and a plain, unassuming style (although one that demonstrates great narrative skill), it is clear why Ransome rapidly became, and has remained, an influential favorite. As he said, "You write not *for* children but for yourself, and if, by good fortune, children enjoy what you enjoy, why then you are a writer of children's books. . . . No special credit to you, but simply thumping good luck."[8]

After more than fifty years, the "Swallows and Amazons" books are still bought and read. They are currently available in paperback in the United Kingdom, and have recently been republished in the United States. *Swallows and Amazons* itself was successfully filmed in 1974, and two of the books, *Coot Club* and *The Big Six,* were merged in a 1986 BBC-TV production. Two collections of Ransome's rare or unpublished writings have recently appeared.

Ransome in many ways created a model for the children's book. As we see in this study, he produced a unified oeuvre that allows children who encounter it to develop over both fictional and actual time. While the books may offer the adult reader nostalgia or a search for Arcadia, they offer the child a child-oriented view of a world different from ours (the books are increasingly period pieces) that couples wish-fulfillment with a practical guide for how to achieve one's wishes. His major legacy has been in the *respect* that subsequent writers have been able to show to children and adults alike. Ransome shared with Carroll, Kipling, and to some extent Nesbit the skill of producing for children a worldview to which they can immediately relate, that is not patronizing, and that sees all skills as equal and as equally interesting.

But it is as well to remember that *Swallows and Amazons* was Ransome's twenty-seventh book (if we include two translations) and that he would, as Kit Pearson puts it, "still have won a place in children's literature for his folk-tale collection *Old Peter's Russian Tales* (1916)."[9] He would also have a permanent place in sailing literature for his account of building a boat and sailing her on the Baltic, *Racundra's First Cruise* (1928); and in the literature of fishing for his essay collections *Rod and Line* (1929) and *Mainly about Fishing* (1959).

The "Swallows and Amazons" series is, then, the work of a polymath. When Ransome returned to the Lake District to write his children's books, he had been a journalist in many exotic places; he had reported the Russian Revolution, played chess with Lenin, and married Trotsky's secretary. He had been sued by Lord Alfred Douglas for slander in his book on Oscar Wilde (Ransome was acquitted), and had lived a cheerful bohemian life in London with writers and poets such as Edward Thomas. His life has interesting parallels with two other major writers about the countryside, William Wordsworth and Richard Jefferies. If great children's books need deep authorial roots, then the "Swallows and Amazons" books certainly qualify.

This study, then, while concentrating on the children's books, also explores Ransome's early life, or lives, and his lesser-known and neglected writings, to discover what skills he brought to children's books. It is remarkable how often the characteristics of the authors he translated or edited emerge, transformed, in his own books. Also, as a prototype literary theorist and folklorist, Ransome understood the mechanics of structure and storytelling, and this understanding is reflected in his structural patterns and narrative techniques. The "Swallows and Amazons" series is approached on the assumption that readers are new to the books. Finally, I consider just what Ransome's influence has been, and what critical judgments can be made on this father of modern British children's literature.

Acknowledgments

My greatest specific debt is to Mr. John Bell, Arthur Ransome's friend and executor, for very kindly allowing me to examine, and to publish for the first time, extracts from Ransome's first story and a photograph of Ransome.

I acknowledge with thanks the kind permission of the Estate of Arthur Ransome and Jonathan Cape Ltd. to publish extracts from Ransome's work. Arthur Ransome's illustrations for the Swallows and Amazons series are reproduced courtesy of Jonathan Cape Limited.

Anyone writing about Arthur Ransome must write in the shadow of two books. The first is Hugh Brogan's exemplary *The Life of Arthur Ransome;* I acknowledge my debt to his scholarship, the extent of which should be obvious from the references. The second is Christina Hardyment's *Arthur Ransome and Captain Flint's Trunk,* the book that every Ransome enthusiast would wish to have written. Although I have largely avoided biographical criticism in this book, Ms. Hardyment's literary detective work cannot be ignored and is greatly appreciated.

I should like to thank those who have helped in other ways: Christopher Sheppard for assisting me at the Brotherton Library at the University of Leeds; the staff at Leeds Central Library; Dennis Butts and Rose Bell for putting me in touch with John Bell; Mary Butts for finding, and Nancy Chambers for lending me, essential texts; Louisa Smith for checking references at 4,000 miles; Nick Hackett for his work on the photograph of Ransome; and my brother Robin, sailor and fisherman in the true Ransome tradition, who introduced me to Ransome's books and whose copy of *We Didn't Mean to Go to Sea,* which I borrowed in 1954, I promise to return shortly.

My editor, Lois Kuznets, deserves an individual paragraph of thanks for producing, under great pressure of time, literally thousands of suggestions, large and small (a few of which I ignored) and for correcting my American.

And, most of all, to my wife, Sarah, for suffering the gestation of another book at the same time as a pregnancy. To her, and to our fourth daughter, Chloë, whose delivery was in the same week as the manuscript, this book is dedicated.

Chronology

1884 Arthur Mitchell Ransome born 18 January, Headingley, Leeds, England.

1893 Attends school at Windermere Old College.

1897 Attends school at Rugby; father dies.

1901 Attends Yorkshire College (later, the University of Leeds).

1902 Moves to London and works as errand boy for the publisher Grant Richards. After six months, leaves and lives as a freelance writer.

1903 Meets W. G. Collingwood (author and partner of John Ruskin) at Coniston.

1904 First book, *The ABC of Physical Culture*. Forms friendship with Edward Thomas. Spends summers in the Lake District. Several minor works. Regular visits to Paris.

1907 *Bohemia in London*.

1909 Marries Ivy Constance Walker. *A History of Storytelling*.

1910 Daughter Tabitha born. *Edgar Allan Poe*.

1911 *The Book of Love; The Hoofmarks of the Faun*.

1912 *Oscar Wilde*. Ransome is sued for libel by Lord Alfred Douglas.

1913 Wins libel case, with costs. *Portraits and Speculations*. Travels to Russia.

1915 *The Elixir of Life*.

1916 Appointed Russian correspondent for the *Daily News*. *Old Peter's Russian Tales*.

1917 Meets Evgenia Petrovna Shelepina, who becomes Trotsky's personal secretary.

1918 Leaves Russia for Sweden. *The Truth about Russia*.

1919 Returns to England; returns to Russia as correspondent for the *Manchester Guardian*. Leaves Russia with Evgenia. *Aladdin*.

1920 Lives in Latvia and Estonia. *The Soldier and Death*.

1921 *The Crisis in Russia*.

1922 Builds *Racundra* and cruises in the Baltic.

1923 *Racundra's First Cruise*.

1924 Divorced from Ivy. Marries Evgenia at Reval, 8 May.

1925 Reports on Egypt for two months. Buys "Low Ludderburn" in the Lake District. Begins to write for the *Manchester Guardian,* including periodical fishing essays "Rod and Line," and others under the pseudonym "William Blunt."

1926 Article on Russia for the *Encyclopaedia Brittanica*. Visits China for the *Manchester Guardian*.

1927 *The Chinese Puzzle*.

1928 Visits Moscow for the *Manchester Guardian*.

1929 Begins *Swallows and Amazons*. Resigns from *Manchester Guardian*. Returns to write Saturday articles, and visits Egypt again. *Rod and Line* (fishing essays reprinted from *Manchester Guardian*).

1930 *Swallows and Amazons*.

1931 *Swallows and Amazons* illustrated by Clifford Webb. Begins *Peter Duck;* writes and publishes *Swallowdale*.

1932 Visits Aleppo. *Peter Duck*.

1933 *Winter Holiday*.

1934 Tours on Norfolk Broads. *Coot Club*. Begins *Pigeon Post*.

1935 Moves to Levington, near Pin Mill on the River Orwell, Suffolk.

1936 Writes resume of *We Didn't Mean to Go to Sea;* finishes pictures for *Swallowdale*. *Pigeon Post*. Sails his cutter, the *Nancy Blackett,* to Flushing (Vlissingen), Holland.

1937 Carnegie Medal. *We Didn't Mean to Go to Sea*.

1939 *Secret Water*.

1940 Printing blocks and some illustrations for *The Big Six* lost in air raid. *The Big Six.* Moves to "The Heald" on Coniston Water.

1941 *Missee Lee.*

1943 *The Picts and the Martyrs.*

1945 Visits the Isle of Lewis for material for *Great Northern?.* Moves to London.

1947 *Great Northern?.*

1948 Moves to "Lowick Hall" (and farm). Writes introduction to Joshua Slocum's *Sailing Alone round the World,* the first of five such introductions for Rupert Hart-Davis's "Mariner's Library."

1949 Buys neighboring farm.

1950 Moves to London, but holidays in the Lake District.

1952 Hon. Litt. D., University of Leeds.

1953 Made Commander of the Order of the British Empire.

1953 Last voyage, in sloop *Lottie Blossom,* to Cherbourg.

1959 *Mainly about Fishing.*

1963 Buys "Hill Top" in the Lake District.

1967 Dies 3 June at Cheadle, near Manchester. Buried at Rusland.

1969 *The Fool of the World and the Flying Ship* (from *Old Peter's Russian Tales*), illustrated by Uri Shulevitz, wins the Caldecott Medal.

1975 Evgenia Ransome dies 19 March.

1976 *Autobiography,* edited by Rupert Hart-Davis.

1984 *The War of the Birds and the Beasts and Other Russian Tales,* edited by Hugh Brogan.

1988 *Coots in the North and Other Stories,* edited by Hugh Brogan.

1

Childhood and Bohemia

Arthur Mitchell Ransome had, after his childhood, three lives. In the first, in Edwardian London, he was a struggling hack writer—gauche, impressionable, pretentious, well-read, and enthusiastic—writing about anything. In the second, he was an expert foreign correspondent, deeply involved in revolutionary Russia, producing reports that made him very unpopular with the British government. In the third, he was a sailor, fisherman, and world-famous writer of children's books. His was an unusual, quirky life, producing an unusual and quirky character: an interesting mixture of the romantic and the pragmatic. His early books, many of them now forgotten, reflect this mixture closely.

If there was any single pervading influence on his life and writing, it is probably the English Lake District. The Lake District formed his childhood; he returned to it during his cosmopolitan existence, yearned for it on his travels, and intermittently lived in it thereafter.

The Lake District, says a recent guide to Britain, is "set like a jewel among the Cumbrian Mountains. There are 16 major lakes [and] towering above them are four mountains topping 3,000 feet, including Scafell Pike, England's highest peak. . . . Its superb scenery is much the same today as when Wordsworth lived there and found inspiration among its hills and lakes."[1] The area has exercised a perennial attraction on both sportsmen and writers, and had a profound influence on a man who was both of those things. Like Wordsworth, Ransome drew his real strengths as a writer from the area and, like Wordsworth, found it to be a restorative place after involvement in revolution.

Arthur Ransome was born in Leeds in 1884, son of a history professor at what was to become the University of Leeds. (As Ransome put it later, "My father was a fisherman who was a professor of history in his spare time.")[2] The city of Leeds is within striking distance of the lake country, and the Ransomes spent their holidays there. Ransome described the early visits in his *Autobiography* with great affection: "We made friends with the farm animals, with the charcoal-burners who in those days still dwelt in wigwams carefully watching their smoking mounds, with the postman, several gamekeepers, several poachers and various fishermen. We took part in the haymaking, turned the butter-churn for Annie Swainson, picked mushrooms and blackberries, tickled trout under the little bridge."[3] Almost everything he mentions surfaces in his most famous books. His description of his "private ritual" each time he arrived at Coniston Water is even more significant: "I used first of all to rush down to the lake. . . . Without letting the others know what I was doing, I had to dip my hand in the water, as a greeting to the beloved lake or as a proof to myself that I had indeed come home" (*A*, 26).

It was a home to which he would return for the rest of his life, and a happy family time that he would re-create in his best books. The Lake District gave him a sense of democracy, as it did Wordsworth (rather more superficially); and the sense that all people and skills are equally valuable suffuses his children's books. When Hugh Shelley wrote his short monograph on Ransome in 1960, he criticized *The Picts and the Martyrs,* one of the books set in the Lake District. "At times," he wrote, "there is an almost feudal atmosphere, for not only parents and other relations join in, but the lower orders play their parts." Ransome, who saw Shelley's manuscript, added a footnote to this: "In the Lake country there are no 'lower orders.'"[4]

On Arthur's fourth birthday, Ransome's father gave him *Robinson Crusoe,* "as a reward for having myself read it from end to end. Thereafter I read voraciously" (*A*, 34). His mother read aloud to the children, with a basic rule that Ransome admired: "She would never read aloud to us a book that she did not enjoy reading herself. . . . Any book worth reading by children is also worth reading by grown-up persons" (*A*, 35). His account of childhood reading is typical of the period: *Holiday House, The Rose and the Ring,* Lear, Carroll, Kingsley, and Marryat; "the whole spectrum of Andrew Lang's fairy books, collected one by one at Christmas and on birthdays"; Ewing, Yonge, Scott, Blackmore, Andersen, the Grimms, *The Jungle Books* "hot from the press." Regarding Ballantyne, "We had . . . *The Young Fur Traders, White Ice,* and *Coral Island.* (My grandmother took me out to tea in a garden where, silently worshipping, I shook hands with Ballantyne in the summer before he went to Italy to die)."[5] Perhaps

THE ISLAND CAMP

most important was W. G. Collingwood's *Thorstein of the Mere* ("a book that we counted peculiarly our own"), part of which was set on Peel Island in Coniston Water, the central location for *Swallows and Amazons*.

His mature comments are very much against "imitation" books— those written for a market or for profit without the engagement of the writer—but he remembered his father's "shocked astonishment when I did not realise that *The Black Arrow* was in comparison [to *Treasure Island*] a poor machine-made thing" (*A*, 36).

As Hugh Brogan, Ransome's biographer, points out, Ransome's attitude to his father was ambivalent. In many ways he worshiped him, whereas the *Autobiography*, perhaps unconsciously, gives a rather less sympathetic picture.[6] This contradiction may well be reflected in his portraits of the benevolent but flawed uncle and the god-like or understanding fathers of the "Swallows and Amazons" series. His relationship to his mother was more straightforward, and he turned to her affectionately throughout his life for reassurance and encouragement. We can search his children's books in vain for a mother figure who is anything but loving and supportive. (This applies to all the women in the "Swallows and Amazons" series. Even the dragonish Great Aunt of *Swallowdale* and *The Picts and the Martyrs* or the astringent Mrs. Tyson of *Pigeon Post* are eventually drawn sympathetically.)

Ransome attributes his career as a writer to an accident:

I was not meant to be a writer at all. I was a cheerful small boy of action . . . when, at about the age of eight, we were all playing at ships under and on an old dining-room table . . . with a heavy iron screw pointing downwards in the middle of it. It was my watch below. . . . Suddenly, somebody . . . raised a shout for "All hands on deck!" I started up. That heavy iron screw made a horrible dent in the top of my skull . . . I crawled out much shaken, played no more that day, but took a small blue notebook and wrote in it my first story, about a desert island. I have been at it ever since.[7]

That first story, written in red ink in a small notebook (a little over one inch square) with a blue cover, is called *The Desert Island*. In just over 1,100 words, the nine-year-old Arthur produced a well-rounded and coherent distillation of Ballantyne and his literary brothers. In the story, Jack's father disappears, and Jack and his friend Tom go aboard a ship "bound for the Friendly Isles." They are shipwrecked; build a stockade; tame a goat, a pig and a "parrakeet"; have pitched battles with hundreds of savages; and are finally rescued by Jack's father.

Two brief extracts printed here for the first time give the flavor of the story:

> They built a house and a stockade round it to keep it safe from wild beasts or savages if any should come. Tom shot a wild duck and a sort of pigeon which lasted for breakfast and dinner and they found some bananas and cocoanuts [*sic*] for tea. There was a little stream running through underneath the stockade so that they should never run short of water. Jack nevertheless took two or three barrels and filled them with water in case the stream dried up. They also gathered a great deal of fruit to preserve because if they were attacked by savages they would not be able to get out to get any. They caught a wild goat which they tamed because as they had no cow they could get its milk.

This is very reminiscent of the fantasy played out by Bevis and Mark in Richard Jefferies's *Bevis*. Ransome, even then, had an eye for fishing: "Two or three days after this happened they went out in their boat to fish. They saw several sharks which were swimming past them and they caught some fish very like our plaice and one like a sea trout."

Being both a poor scholar and bad at sports, Ransome had, at least initially, unhappy schooldays. When he was at last diagnosed as myopic, he went on to have at least a passable time at Rugby school. He returned to Leeds to attend college (to study applied science) but, after less than a year, gave up and went to London to seek his fortune as a writer, beginning as an office boy in the firm of Grant Richards in 1901.

This was a London that looked to Paris for its "bohemian" ways, a London of small cafes and bars and small publishers and magazines. Rather like Kenneth Grahame before him[8] and like A. A. Milne, who came to London and was appointed assistant editor of *Punch* in 1906, Ransome was entranced.

Writing anything from fairy-tales to reviews, Ransome took to the "bohemian" life and met, among many others, E. Nesbit, Cecil Chesterton (G. K.'s brother), John Masefield, and many of the minor literati of the period. He shared a flat with the poet Edward Thomas, often surviving only on cheese and apples, occasionally sharing brief riches, and sometimes burning the review copies of books for warmth. "I kept alive," he wrote later, "and continued my education by running errands and packing up parcels in an office, and writing the most terrible rubbish when I got home. . . . A year later I was selling my rubbish and making some sort of living by it."[9]

The prevailing fin de siècle atmosphere of London was one of high artiness mixed with escapism, often toward an imagined rural paradise, and with more than a tinge of fashionable paganism. All of this reached its apotheosis in *The Wind in the Willows,* and the whimsicality that accompanied it also surfaced in *Winnie-the-Pooh.* Equally fashionable was the bohemian atmosphere, with its posing and "precious" living—an atmosphere epitomized by Oscar Wilde.

From 1904 onwards, Ransome traveled to Paris frequently and taught himself French. His account of this time, although written in old age, gives a very clear impression of a rather nervously egocentric youth: "I think I should confess that I never did learn French, to talk it as it should be talked, but I learnt to read it as easily as English, and to rattle away in a language the French understood and that later Remy de Gourmont, Paul Fort and even Anatole France used to forgive" (*A,* 120).

Even as a young man, Ransome was well-read and a book collector in a small way, yet surprisingly his early output was undistinguished and derivative, and he did not capitalize on his country background.

During his time in London, he spent whatever holidays he could in the Lake District, meeting the poet Lascelles Abercrombie and, more importantly, W. G. Collingwood. Collingwood had written not only a standard history of and guide to the Lake District but also one of Ransome's childhood favorites, *Thorstein of the Mere.* Collingwood had two daughters, Barbara and Dora (who taught Ransome to sail), and a son, R. G. (Robin) Collingwood, who became a distinguished philosopher. Ransome became one of the family. Barbara, having turned down the romantic Arthur's proposal, later married a notable geologist, Oscar Gnospellius (to whom *Pigeon Post* is dedicated), while, most important for literary history, Dora married Ernest Altounyan, and had five children who were the initial models for the Walker family in *Swallows and Amazons.*

Ransome deepened his knowledge of the lake country, camping, sailing, fishing, and getting to know the local people; the charcoalburners, for example, would bake clay pipes for him. But it does not seem to have occurred to him to make use of the material around him. Rather, he produced anything that would sell. "The only excuse for those early books," he wrote, "is that they were written (and unfortunately published) at a time when I should have been a university student and saved from myself by the laughter of my fellows. Instead, I was keeping myself alive by selling what should have been mere exercises. It surprises me that I was able to sell them" (*A,* 101).

Even the most sympathetic modern reader might concur. The first piece is a very rare volume, *The ABC of Physical Culture* (1904), of which Ransome noted, rather endearingly, "I can remember patting its silly little cover much as I have patted a boat when she and I have been alone at sea and struggling along in unkindly weather" (*A*, 100–1). He followed this with two collections of essays, *The Souls of the Streets and Other Little Papers* (1904) and *The Stone Lady* (1905), which even his usually supportive biographer, Hugh Brogan, describes as "not only trite, but sickeningly sentimental."[10]

The Souls of the Streets is the earliest of his quasi-mystical pagan excursions. The title of the eponymous piece is intended to be taken literally: "I can remember when I first let myself be convinced that there really was a hidden life beneath the bricks and mortar." Parts of his writing are reminiscent of Chesterton, but many others have a coyness that is not easy to swallow: "Trouble not with mine but remember your own sweet visions." "Two Tramps," a rather patronizing piece in which the narrator joins "companions . . . tramps like myself" bears very little relationship to real life in the real countryside. "A Girl in Spring" is a very sensual and, as Ransome would have admitted, adolescent conjuring of the season as a girl, who is given to spontaneous (and pointless) laughter.[11]

As the title and subtitle suggest, *The Stone Lady: Ten Little Papers and Two Mad Stories,* is in much the same vein. The "little papers" are mostly sketches; some are whimsical (the title piece is about two children cleaning the face of a statue); some are in the occasional-essay tradition epitomized by Jerome K. Jerome's *Idle Thoughts of an Idle Fellow* ("The Great Downtrodden" is about boots); and some are mystical/romantic ("Vision of Spring in Autumn"). The two stories are equally uneven. "Meddling with the Fairies" is a satire about adult unbelievers, while "Incense Burners" is a fantasy about a ruthless sect of priests, somewhat reminiscent of the early surrealist work of Dylan Thomas.[12]

Other books written at this period were small books on nature for children and the ominously titled *Highways and Byways in Fairyland* (1906). All of these books (probably to Ransome's relief) eventually virtually disappeared from sight; after all, apprentice work can hardly be held against a writer. But the next book he wrote is still in print and tells us a great deal not only about its author but about the world in which he lived.

Ransome called *Bohemia in London* "the first book I wrote that was not altogether a makeshift" (*A*, 113). It was suggested to him by an acquaintance, Stefana Stevens, who said, "There's a book that ought to be written, and you are the one who ought to write it, a book on Bohemia in London, an essayistical sort of book, putting Bohemia of today against a background of the past" (*A*, 114). Ransome finished it by the end of the summer of 1907, and it was well received; the *Daily Telegraph,* for example, described it as "a book . . . of the brave days when all the world is twenty-one, when all the year is spring" (25 September 1907). In the *Autobiography,* Ransome says, "It was praised far beyond its deserts and at great length. . . . I was twenty-two when I began that book, twenty-three when I finished it, but no-one could have guessed that from the book, which is written almost as if from a great distance I were looking back on my own youth. It has much rubbish in it but is not wholly bad, though I should be sorry if it were to be reprinted" (*A*, 114–16).

But reprinted it has been, by the Oxford University Press in 1984. Rupert Hart-Davis had suggested republication in 1950 and had given the book to David Garnett for review. Garnett felt that the book had a certain charm, and commented, "It is an odd book—full of genuine feeling and understanding which lapses frequently into rather trashy journalism. . . . It is a mixture of sensibility and commonsense crossed with immature romanticism. . . . It is not a book to add lustre to Ransome's name—it is a young, immature and absurd book."[13]

To the unbiased reader, Garnett errs on the side of generosity. *Bohemia in London* is an unconsciously pretentious book about rather more consciously pretentious people. It reads now, unwittingly, as a satirical comment on a society of artists and intellectuals, a society that, one might skeptically suspect, has changed little since Ransome's time.

The book is episodic: Ransome describes his arrival in London and his encounters with writers and artists. Enthusiastic and naive, he seems intent on appearing as another Chesterton, weighty, wise, and paradoxical. Unfortunately he is too close to his material, and would-be bacchanalia tend to collapse into the bathos of "That was a great night" or "How we laughed." It would not be to Ransome's credit to quote much of this part of the book.

The narrative is interspersed with material that conjures up Johnson and Goldsmith, Milton and Chaucer, and other ghosts of the London streets, and in parts, Ransome does manage to generate a period charm—the more, perhaps, because it is lost to us. For example:

> Far down on the Fetter Lane side of the street there is the Cheshire Cheese, still the dirty-fronted, low-browed tavern, with stone flasks in the window, that it was even before Johnson's time. Here, so people say, Johnson and Goldsmith used to sup and be merry with their friends. . . . It is a pleas-

ant brown room, this, in the tavern, with Johnson's portrait hanging on the wall, old wooden benches beside good solid tables, and a homely smell of toasted cheese. (*BL,* 162–63)

Ransome is at his best when dealing with the actual, rather than the fanciful. The drunken undergraduate antics that he describes with a spurious air of distance also cast a good deal of doubt on the status of the "illustrious" predecessors to these bohemians. The best that can be said of the book is said by Brogan: "The book clearly foreshadows Ransome's journalism, which is chiefly distinguished by its ability to convey, vividly, clearly and economically, what it felt like to be among certain people at a certain place and moment."[14] But equally it shows Ransome as a bookman who loved and respected a literary tradition. This characteristic emerges in his later children's books, where he was to emphasize the influence that such a tradition has.

In 1907 he began a series of books, "The World's Story Tellers," for the publishers T. C. and E. C. Jack. Ransome wrote an introductory essay on each writer and collected (and generally translated) the stories. In 1909 he gathered the introductions (with some extra essays) into *A History of Storytelling: Studies in the Development of Narrative,* illustrated by Jessie Gavin (another young woman—among many—with whom Ransome was in love during this period). This book shows him to have been no mean critic, even if the frame of the book (completed when he was still only twenty-five) has traces of his sub-Chestertonian manner. His idea, as he says in the preface, was "[to] take here a book and there a book . . . suggested mainly by the masterpieces I love."[15] His selection, and, more important, what he chooses to say about the writers, gives a very telling indication of Ransome's own directions and energies, although we should heed his warning that "it is too easy to construct a man out of his work. It is more interesting to compare the man of this world with the man he would have liked to be, and the man he chose to express" (*HS,* 236).

He ranges over both English and French authors and over a long timespan. This eclecticism may well have contributed, in these more academically compartmentalized days, to the book's current obscurity, while contemporary books of similar tone, such as those by Professor Sir Walter Raleigh (*The English Novel,* 1894) or Professor George Saintsbury (*A Short History of English Literature,* 1898) have been more accessible.

Ransome begins in much the same self-conscious manner as in *Bohemia in London*—"This is a spring day, and I am writing in a flood of sunlight in front of a brown French inn"—and proceeds in the same tone:

> A book that calls itself a history of a subject with as many byways and blind alleys as exist in the history of story-telling, is precisely the kind of book that one would wish one's enemy to have written. . . . And now that it is done, I think of it sadly enough. It should have been so beautiful. When I see an old church, like the priory church at Cartmel, standing grey and solemn in the mist above the houses, or hear an old song, like "Summer is icumen in" . . . I feel that these things have meant more to man than battles. These are his dreams and his ideals, resting from age to age . . . recorded each in its own way, in stone, in melody . . . and in the tales also that, changing continually, have "held children from play and old men from the chimney-corner." (*HS*, vii, ix)

Ransome touches the sagas, the *Mabinogion,* and *Aucassin and Nicolette,* and then moves rapidly on to *The Romance of the Rose,* Chaucer, Boccaccio, the early "rogue novel" such as *Lazarillo de Tormes* (1553), Nash's *The Unfortunate Traveller* (1594), Le Sage's *Gil Blas* (1715–35), and Cervantes.

His judgments, which generally follow Saintsbury, are not striking, and he achieves much of Saintsbury's elegant and judicious tone. The following description of Defoe's style could easily be transposed to describe Ransome's own in his later books: "His style is as simple and effective as a bricklayer's hod. He carries facts in it, and builds with them alone. The resulting books are like solid Queen Anne houses. There is no affectation about them . . . but they are very good for 'matter-of-fact readers' to live in" (*HS,* 135).

A History of Storytelling, then, is a rich sourcebook for the influences on Ransome's own mature style. Despite his affectations of manner, he favors the writers who are simple and robust, and is not happy with Richardson, finding, conventionally, that "Pamela's respectability is a little disgusting" (*HS* 145). His approach, perhaps a little too obviously "manly" and frank, sits well with the biographical evidence of his liking for male pastimes, good walks, and good inns. It is perhaps unsurprising that Sterne only appears in a footnote, for Ransome, when he found his true voice, was very much a plain storyteller. However, Ransome's range of reference allows him to make very illuminating comparisons. For example: "For the story of the three generations of the giants, Rabelais needed land and sea, Paris and Touraine. For the adventures of his strolling players, Scarron needed a dozen little towns along the Loire, with inns and chateaux and what not. But for the adventures of Humanity, Sterne, who learnt from both of them, needed only a bowling-green, a study, a bedroom, and a parlour" (*HS*, 170).

The second part of the book follows romanticism into Europe. Ransome looks at Chateaubriand, considers the influence of Scott on Hugo, Balzac, and Dumas, and quotes Horace Walpole that "the great resources of fancy had been dammed up by a strict adherence to common life" (*HS*, 189).

Ransome's portraits of the French romantics have immense energy. Dumas, for example, creates characters who "are all alive, not with an independent, almost hostile existence like that of the characters of Balzac, but with a vitality they owe to their creator and to us, the free coursing blood of boyish dreams" (*HS*, 212). Ransome seems to approach Hugo with more caution and perhaps more reverence, seeing him as a more complex craftsman, whereas his vigorous portrait of Balzac reflects something of the part that Ransome liked to take himself.

There are other intriguing sidelights. When he is discussing Gautier, for example, a passage calls to mind immediately the atmosphere of the Far East that Ransome later so successfully created in the children's book *Missee Lee:* "The East is not an expression of philosophy, or of geography, but of temperament. . . . Men have fallen in love with it. . . . It has been given the compelling power of a religion" (*HS*, 232).

His images of Scott's writing are both apposite and redolent of his own background: "The sensation of reading a Waverley Novel is that of leaning on the parapet of a bridge on a summer day, watching the sunlight on a twig that lies motionless in a backwater. The day is so calm and the sunlight so pleasant that we continue watching the twig for a time quite disproportionate to the interest we feel in it. . . . He saw life, as a short-sighted man sees a landscape, in its essentials. . . . Humanity. . . . moves through his pages like a stout wind over a northern moor" (*HS*, 194, 197). Scott's writing was, of course, the antithesis of the mature Ransome's, but perhaps close to that of the young man.

Among the Americans, Ransome praises Hawthorne's gentleness and love of nature, but also finds him a "provincial pedant" (*HS*, 264). Although Poe, too, seems an unlikely member of Ransome's parade of forceful, bluff, manly writers, Ransome's glowing account derives partly from a fascination with the "hothouse" or grotesque aspects of Poe (he found similar material in Wilde) and even more from his interest in Poe's craftsmanship.

As a critic—and, later, as a writer—Ransome was fascinated by the technicalities of the writer's craft. How were stories successfully con-

structed? Exploring these questions in the context of Poe, he quotes
Hazlitt on Godwin's *Caleb Williams* and says, "There can be no doubt
that in *Caleb Williams* we see the beginnings of self-conscious construction in story-telling" (*HS,* 244). In his enthusiasm to make a
point, Ransome seems to have forgotten Fielding, Sterne, and many
others, but he quotes Godwin himself (from the later editions of
Caleb Williams) with clear approval: "I formed a conception of a book
of fictitious adventure that should in some way be distinguished by
a very powerful interest. Pursuing this idea, I invented first the third
volume of my tale, then the second, and last of all the first" (*HS,* 245).

Rupert Hart-Davis, Ransome's friend and executor, notes in the introduction to the *Autobiography,* "It was his habit to prepare an extremely detailed synopsis, complete with chapter-titles, so that he
knew exactly what was to happen in each chapter. He then began
writing whichever chapter took his fancy or seemed easiest, leaving
the most difficult to last" (*A,* 9).

Discussing Poe, Ransome quotes a passage that he himself eventually took to heart and that could have referred to the "Swallows
and Amazons" books: "In the whole composition there should be no
word written, of which the tendency, direct or indirect, is not to the
one pre-established design. And by such means, with such care and
skill, a picture is at length painted which leaves in the mind of him
who contemplates it with a kindred art a sense of the fullest satisfaction" (*HS,* 246). (These passages reappear in his critical work on
Poe. In the introduction to that book, Ransome refers to the "few sen-
tences . . . taken from a previous short essay" and defends this recy-
cling with the somewhat abrupt statement, "There seemed to be no
sufficient reason for obscuring by a paraphrase what was as clear as
I could make it.")[16]

If Poe is Ransome's yardstick for structure, then Mérimée is one of
his mentors for style, and he begins enthusiastically, "There is a lean,
athletic air about the tales of Prosper Mérimée (*HS,* 273). He
goes on:

> Mérimée gives his tales no more background than an En-
> glishman could put without immodesty into an after-dinner
> conversation. He does not decorate them with words, nor try
> to suggest atmosphere by rhythm or any other of the subtler
> uses of language. . . . His style is without felicities . . . but its
> limitations are its virtues. Pomp is the ruin of a plain fact
> as of a plain man, and rhetoric rolls facts along too fast to
> do anything but smooth them. This style, that seems to dis-
> claim any pretension to be a style at all, leaves facts unen-
> cumbered, with their corners unpolished. . . . Always when

reading Mérimée, I have an impression of listening to a man who has seen the world, and was young once upon a time. (*HS*, 277–78)

Again, this could be a self-portrait of the older Ransome.

A History of Storytelling gives the impresssion of a man whose preferred writers are those whose virtues of style he would eventually follow: plain prose, careful structure, and a vigorous and straightforward attitude to life.

While completing *A History of Storytelling,* Ransome embarked on his unhappy first marriage. Ivy Walker was attractive, dramatic, and emotionally unstable, and for Ransome the next four years, before he escaped to Russia, were traumatic. Nevertheless, he continued to write, and a full-length critical work, *Edgar Allen Poe, a Critical Study,* published by Martin Secker in 1910, was sandwiched between two anthologies, *The Book of Friendship* (1909) and *The Book of Love* (1911).

These are both beautifully produced volumes, each containing well over a hundred items, with an emphasis on the classics and the romantics. *The Book of Friendship* is dedicated to Lascelles Abercrombie and makes one of the earliest references to Ransome's love of the Lake District: "I would give many meals to meet that man again on Lowick Bridge and walk with him to the Hark to Melody [an inn]; and I send him this book in memory of those old walks and talks and pleasant inn parlours."[17] *The Book of Love* is similar, with a romantic (and perhaps wishful) introduction, describing the process of selecting and copying the extracts, under the old apple tree "shading a heavy wooden table" where "Bees hum above the copyist's head and butterflies perch sometimes upon the ink-bottle."[18]

The Poe study is in Ransome's rather florid early manner, and can best be summed up in part of his own summary of Poe's work: "His work, as it is left to us, is made up of observations and finds, by the way, each one modified by the blind alley, high road, or field path that he happened to be pursuing at the time. It is embedded in rubbish and beautiful things, verse with the jewelled wings of tropic moths, hoarse-throated critical articles calming again and again into passages of invaluable wisdom" (*P*, 215).

The book is based on the interesting premise that "Poe's brain was more stimulating than his art, and that the tales and poems by which he is known were but the by-products of an unconcluded search" (*P*, ix). He places Poe on a level with some of his own favorite critics, Hazlitt, Leigh Hunt, Lamb, and Lowell (*P*, 47); but, as he observes, "England and America needed differently built reviewers," and Poe's criticism is "without charm" (*P*, 48, 49).

Often it may seem that Ransome's choice of Poe rests in a certain sympathy for the writer forced to write below his best. Winnowing Poe's collected criticism, he says: "There is no need to judge a man's aim by those occasions on which Forced Haste, an unfriendly hand, pulls his arm aside at the moment of loosing the arrow, or sends the shaft on its way before his eye is steady on the target" (P, 55). A similar fellow feeling appears in matters of technique. He quotes Poe's *Marginalia*, "It is the curse of a certain order of mind, that it can never rest satisfied with the consciousness of its ability to do a thing. It must both know and show how it was done," and adds, in a moment of self-revelation: "The man who is as interested in the way of doing a thing as in the thing when done, is the man who is likely to put a new tool into the hands of his fellow-craftsmen" (P, 63). This was precisely what Ransome did for a generation of children's writers. His interest in the craft of writing for children raised its status; his validation of practical activity as a source of intrinsic excitement encouraged its use in many later books.

His work on Poe's poetry, as on poetry in general, is less sure, and he is inclined to praise what many critics would now regard as vapid. But his praise of Poe's analytical faculties, which laid upon him "the curse of self-consciousness for which we value him most highly," looks at tales like *The Murders in the Rue Morgue* and *The Purloined Letter*, and shows clear enjoyment of the architecture of plotting: "The true artist is he who is able to . . . baffle the inquisitive reader asking which lines were first imagined, who is able, that is to say, to preserve an absolute unity between the nucleus and its elaboration" (P, 71). He seems also to admire Poe "because of his tendency to the segregation of particular moods of his mind. . . . He, at bottom a critic and thinker, wore several masks in turn" (P, 161).

This book contrasts sharply with *The Hoofmarks of the Faun* (1911), of which the best that might be said is that it is thoroughly of its time. Both the sensuality of Wilde and the cynicism of Poe influenced his style, together with fashionable pseudo-paganism. It is difficult for the contemporary reader to decide which aspect makes the more uncomfortable reading.

"The Silver Snakes", for example (written in 1905), an overblown anecdote about a mad painter, makes an attempt at Wildean sensuality: "He took a liqueur bottle, and a new box of cigarettes, and lit the lamp and candles in the recess. He poured out a slender glass of an amber liqueur, that shone with purple shadows as he held it to the light, sipped it and lit a cigarette. . . . When the room was as hot as an orchid—he dropped the cigarette behind the grate and vehemently, even furiously, threw his dressing-gown aside. The slim, green book was in his hand. He kissed it, pressing his lips to the smooth leather as to a woman's skin."[19] Well, perhaps it would not be charitable to continue, nor to speculate too closely on the theme of failed dreams and dislike between married partners in "The Footways of Dream" (1911), dedicated to his wife.

But perhaps most characteristic of the stories—and of the period— is the title piece, which begins in quite a different tone: "Under Raven Crag, in the North Country, there is a grey farm with a huge granary built close under the fell, where the meadows give way to rock and bracken on one side and deep woodland on the other" (*HF,* 11). However, this imagery soon collapses into a very precious playfulness. To remember that this was "romance" directed at adults, not children, may give some comfort to those who respect the perceptiveness of children: "His were the dryads of the oaks and the swimming naiads of the green pools and the small goat-footed fauns with silky ears who sported in the vineyards. Often a dryad had kissed his ruddy cheeks, and more than once a naiad had kissed him on the lips, rising from the green depths of her pool when he dipped his mouth in it to drink. But he was held dearest by a faun, a little goat-foot laughing creature who played bo-peep with him behind a tree, and led him jolly dances" (*HF,* 12).

Even Richard Jefferies, at his considerable worst in *Wood Magic,* did not perpetrate anything quite so soporific. The most interesting piece in the book is a memoir of an obscure writer, Peter Swainson, whom Ransome met in London, and who seemed to epitomize the bohemian life, and perhaps, by his name, to remind Ransome of the lake country. Brogan calls this book "a collection of bad, fanciful stories."[20] Nevertheless, *The Hoofmarks of the Faun* is worth remembering as a characteristic part of the undergrowth of writing at the beginning of the century—and as an indication of the immature side of Ransome's character, which the problems of his marriage to Ivy were to help eradicate.

His next publication was a translation of Remy de Gourmont's *A Night in Luxembourg,* an experimental book ideally suited to Ransome's tastes at the time. Ransome himself described it as "crystalline epicureanism."[21]

His involvement with the literary establishment of the time was sharply demonstrated by his next piece of criticism: *Oscar Wilde: A Critical Study,* published by Methuen in 1912 (and "First published at 1s net in 1913"). It was dedicated to Robert Ross (Wilde's literary executor), and the second edition begins with this note, dated May 1913:

The publication of this book in 1912 was the subject of a libel action which was brought against me in the King's Bench

Division of the High Court of Justice, and was heard before
Mr Justice Darling and a Special Jury on four days in April
1913. In that action a verdict was given in my favour. In
bringing out this new edition I have considered the question
of reprinting the book in its original form, as I have a perfect
right to do, but as I do not consider that the passages com-
plained of are essential to the critical purpose of my book I
have decided, in order to spare the feelings of those who
might be pained by the further publication of those passages, to omit them from this edition.[22]

In short, Ransome had been sued by the litigious Lord Alfred Douglas, who claimed that Ransome had suggested that he was responsible for Wilde's downfall. After a dramatic trial, Ransome was
exonerated, but it was a very wearing experience for him.

All that remains of the offending material, in the second edition, is
a bald sentence, sandwiched between the dates of publication of "The
Truth of Masks" and "Lord Arthur Savile's Crime": "In 1886 he began
that course of conduct that was to lead to his downfall" (OW, 30); and
the simple statement, without any comment, that Wilde was eventually prosecuted "on a more serious charge" (OW, 32).

Ransome's reasons for discussing Wilde's life at all are interesting,
especially now that biography is being relegitimized as a critical tool.
"I wished," he writes, "at first, to write a book on Wilde's work in
which no mention of the man or his tragedy should have a place. . . .
I was wrong, of course" (OW, 10). His justification, although expressed somewhat poetically, would form a trenchant attack on the
"text only" schools of criticism. Citing the headnotes that Wordsworth
and others provided to their poems, he comments:

There is a crudity about such obvious assistance, and it
would be quite insufficient without the knowledge on which
we draw unconsciously as we read. But the crudity of those
pitiable little scraps of information is not so remarkable as
that of the presumptuous attempt to read a book as if it has
fallen like manna from heaven, and that of the gross dull-
ness of perception that can allow a man to demand of a poem
or a picture that it shall itself compel him fully to understand it. To gain the privilege of a just appreciation of a
man's books (if, indeed, such an appreciation is possible) we
must know what place they took in his life, and handle the
rough material that dictated even their most ethereal tissue.
(OW, 12)

Wilde, he notes, said that "he put his genius into his life, keeping only his talent for his books," and biography was necessary: "I therefore changed my original intention, and, while concerned throughout with Wilde as artist and critic rather than as criminal, read his biographers and talked with his friends that I might be so far from forgetting as continually to perceive behind the books the spectacle of the man . . . with his strange and brilliant personality" (*OW,* 13).

Ransome devotes five chapters to a shrewd and well-researched assessment of Wilde and then returns, in chapter 8, to the "disaster." Wilde's unnamed vice, Ransome intones, "needs none but a pathological explanation. It was a disease, a malady of the brain, not the necessary consequence of a delight in classical literature" (*OW,* 168). He concludes the very brief chapter with the disclaimer that "an elaborate account of the various trials would in no way serve the purpose of this book" (*OW,* 170).

His attempt to assess Wilde's influence is judicious, but also judiciously vague, for one writing so close to the events. "It is already clear that Wilde has an historical importance too easily underestimated. His indirect influence is incalculable, for his attitude in writing gave literature new standards of valuation" (*OW,* 20). Here we can detect a certain padding and uncertainty, and a sample of Ransome's more pretentious flourishes will serve for the whole: "No man's life was crossed by Wilde's without experiencing a change. Men lived more vividly in his presence, and talked better than themselves. No common man lives and dies without altering, to some extent, the life about him and so the history of the world. How much wider is their influence who live their lives like flames" (*OW,* 21).

Ransome still tends to pose as an elder sage. His comment on Wilde's taking a First Class in Classical Moderations that this is "always a sufficient proof of sound learning" comes from a man who did not go to university. Elsewhere, his decisions have insight and have generally been borne out by later critical opinion. He wrote of "The Canterville Ghost" that it "is just so boisterous as to miss its balance" (*OW,* 88); of *The House of Pomegranates,* that "Wilde wrote with the pen of Flaubert, stories that might have been imagined by Andersen" (*OW,* 96); and of *The Picture of Dorian Gray,* which was first written for a magazine, that "six chapters were added to it to make it long enough for publication as a novel, because those who buy books, like those who buy pictures, are unable to distinguish between size and quality, and imagine that value depends upon area. . . . These circumstances partly explain the lack of proportion, and of cohesion, that mars, though it does not spoil, the first French novel to be written in the English language" (*OW,* 101).

Most interestingly, he ventures into literary theory more than once. Discussing the change in Wilde's manner after his imprisonment, Ransome feels that "a distinction between decoration and realism, though it immediately suggests itself, is too blunt to enable us to state clearly a change in Wilde's writing that it is impossible to overlook" (*OW*, 200). To refine this idea, he takes the concepts of kinetic and potential energy and applies them to language. Literature combines the actual and the potential; ordinary prose is merely actual, whereas music perhaps expresses the purely potential. (He also discusses this theory in *Portraits and Speculations* [1913]). For Wilde, therefore, "decoration was . . . a mode of potentiality" (*OW*, 203); "potentiality" was suggestion, and decoration was its objective correlative.

There are two self-revelatory comments. Of the plays, Ransome notes, "Wilde was never without the power, shared by all amateurs of genius, of using up the odds and ends from one pastime to fill out the detail of another" (*OW*, 148). Of the "very marred stories" in *The Happy Prince and Other Tales* he notes, significantly, "The rest . . . are tales whose morals are a little too obvious even for grown-up people. Children are less willing to be made good" (*OW*, 92).

This book demonstrates the side of Ransome that would have aspired to being a scholar as well as a practical man. The same might be said of *Portraits and Speculations,* the most mature work of this period, published by Macmillan in 1913 and dedicated to the later poet laureate, John Masefield. Apart from essays on Pater and Nietzsche, this book was compiled from earlier essays, and those on Daudet and Coppée were originally prefaces to collections of their stories, published by Black.

The same tone of self-importance still sounds, but his discussion of art shows his awareness of fundamental literary problems: "It would be a fascinating task to show that the too faithful imitation of external things is an impediment to the highest functions of art, and on the other hand, that imitation in some kind, in some degree, is an essential part of that function."[23] This kind of thinking is at the root of the "realism" that appears in the "Swallows and Amazons" series and influences its underlying moral drive: "No artist, no human being, escapes morality, and the code of values that is his will be one of the determining influences on the artist's vision of life" (*PS*, 20).

Portraits and Speculations also rather engagingly mixes wide reading with a down-to-earth style ("Now Kant said . . ." [*PS*, 10]) and a transparent delight in the literary life; in his essay on Aloysius Bertrand, Ransome notes, "M. Anatole France was good enough to direct me in my search for information" (*PS*, 38). The subjects of the essays range from the famous (Daudet, Nietzsche, Pater) to the less well-known (Remy de Gourmont, the symbolist Yone Noguchi).

Ransome was clearly attracted to the vitality of Daudet, an attraction that draws out some interesting observations on childhood and writing about childhood: "One kind of happiness is a childish enjoyment of everything that may occur. Children run about all day, without forethought, and play at being all sorts of things, and chatter and fall asleep, still chattering, in the middle of a sentence. They wake next morning to perform a variation ever so blithe on yesterday's performance.... Daudet's writing was always a means of living for him.... Far from envying that boy of whom he writes, [he] seems to be still identical with him, and tells his escapades as if they were yesterday's, as indeed they might be" (*PS*, 60, 62).

The essay on "Kinetic and Potential Speech," originally published in *The Oxford and Cambridge Review* (and, as we have seen, parts of which also appeared in *Oscar Wilde*), is the most important in the collection. After a preamble that is less florid than usual, Ransome borrows terminology from physics in order to try to define literature: "Kinetic energy is force actually exerted. Potential energy is force that a body is in a position to exert.... I wish to define literature, or rather the medium of literature, as a combination of kinetic with potential speech. In this combination the two are coincident. There is no such thing in literature as speech purely kinetic or purely potential. Purely kinetic speech is prose, not good prose, not literature, but colourless prose" (*PS*, 211).

Ransome is here exploring the distinction later seen as being between literary and functional discourse, although he does not have the linguistic equipment to distinguish the markers that separate the two types. Characteristically, his first example is the sea song, in which he suggests that although the words are worthless, the combination with music makes them memorable: "The words and the melody respectively represent kinetic and potential speech" (*PS*, 212). Ransome's is a very modern critical voice, for with a democratic eye he dismisses the ideologically based classification of texts: "An adoption of the definition of literature that this essay upholds would make ridiculous the classification of books by their subjects and of writers by their opinions, on which so many intellects have wasted time and vitality worthy of more profitable employment" (*PS*, 225).

At this point, around 1913, there was a major change in Ransome's life. He had developed an interest in Russian folk-tales. "In the London Library," he writes in the *Autobiography*, "I had come across Ralston's *Russian Folk Tales* and, while disliking what seemed to me the unsuitable 'literary' prose in which they were written, saw what rich material was there. . . . I had made up my mind to learn enough Russian to be able to read Russian folklore in the original and to tell those stories in the simple language that they seemed to need" (*A*, 157).

He had a more pragmatic reason. His marriage was deteriorating rapidly, despite his affection for his daughter, Tabitha, who had been born in 1910. His wife, according to Brogan, was becoming more hysterical and given to fantasies and violence. (Brogan's biography, although undoubtedly sympathizing with Arthur, portrays Ivy through the evidence of Tabitha and many impartial witnesses.) Ransome's *Autobiography* is very restrained on the subject of his marriage, but he was clearly embittered for the rest of his life. It is not for the literary critic to speculate on the extent to which his children's books were a compensation for the estrangement from his daughter.

And so, although he claimed to be no linguist, in May 1913 Ransome took ship to Denmark on his way to Russia—to a new literary phase of his life.

2

Russia, Revolution, and *Racundra*

Ransome went to St. Petersburg and settled down to live cheaply and to learn Russian from school primers. He wrote an unsuccessful "guide" to St. Petersburg, and began to read folk-tales.

Two short stories, one of which seems to mark a watershed, survive from this period. They have been reprinted by Hugh Brogan in *Coots in the North and Other Stories* (1988).[1] "Ankou" from the *English Review,* 1914 (*CN,* 294–301), is a sombre tale of two old men in a Breton fishing village who are waiting to die. The one who dies last in the year becomes, for the following year, the "Ankou," "who summons in various ways the souls of those who are about to die. . . . The living are so few, a handful of men among the hosts of dead. The dead have been increasing always. To be Ankou of the smallest village is to rule a shadowy multitude" (*CN,* 72, 73).

The spare manner of telling looks forward very much to Ransome's first major work, *Old Peter's Russian Tales* (1916), and the folk-tale element may have provided an earthy discipline that purified Ransome's style. Here is no ornateness or overblown speculation. The idea of two old men trying to outlive each other, but not the year, seems to be above the hothouse perfervidness of, say, *The Hoofmarks of the Faun.* There is sufficient horror in the starkness of the tale.

"The Shepherd's Pipe" (1916), marks a symbolic shift in Ransome's thinking. This Russian story is told, by a middle-aged country gentleman, to a narrator who in the first paragraph begins to sound suspiciously like the young Ransome: "From behind the barn the sounds came, a low whistling melody, the high notes of which were very clear, the low notes marked by the same throaty vibration. Up and

down the scale ran the melody, now and again seeming to turn into
a kind of intimate dialogue between one key and another." But almost
immediately the tone changes. The Russian gentleman says, "'You
are thinking of the shepherds of Arcady . . . the golden age, nymphs,
satyrs, and the rest of them. . . .' 'Something of the kind,' I said. 'If
you keep such things in your head, you will see very little of Russia.
The romantic shepherd does not exist. Scamps, thieves, the terror of
the peasants. . . . No, there is no romance in a shepherd, but as much
rascality and downright wickedness and malice as the devil knows
how to stuff into his skin'" (*CN,* 61–62).

An economical and dramatic tale follows, of a strong young shepherd, who, after being refused the hand of the daughter of the head
man of the village (the Starosta), sets fire to the Starosta's house and
destroys the village. The villagers turn on him and nearly kill him,
and he ends by living as an animal: "He has lived with the beasts
ever since. No one disturbs him. He understands what is said to him,
but never speaks. The servants leave food for him in the cattlesheds.
That is the story of your Theocritan shepherd" (*CN,* 71).

Russia had given Ransome the opportunity to turn his back on the
precious and trivial, and to touch his real roots, the ordinary country
people, through their own stories.

He had, nevertheless, a last fling at romance. He produced a version of *Aladdin,* which was not published until 1920, in what Brogan
calls "pantomime verse."[2] The book has very striking color plates in
the Beardsley manner, and the verse is at best workmanlike. The
dedication, to Lascelles Abercrombie, gives the flavor:

> You are a poet. I my nose
> Grind at the humbler wheel of prose,
> But now and then I make a stanza . . .
> What's that you say? It does not scan, sir . . .
> And though it's not high poetry
> Lascelles its [*sic*] good enough for me.[3]

In 1915 he also completed his first full-length "novel," *The Elixir
of Life.* This book is a pleasant surprise; it shows how far Ransome's
skills as a writer had developed and, incidentally, where he found his
models. Set in 1716, it is the first-person narrative of a young and
foppish philosopher, Richard Stanborough, left to seek his fortune in
the world. He is taken up by John Killigrew, who has discovered the
elixir of life. For the last two hundred years Killigrew has been rejuvenating himself by drinking the elixir, and rejuvenating the elixir
itself by a long series of murders. With the help of Killigrew's "ward,"
Rose ("a daughter of the Gods"), Stanborough resists the temptation

to drink the elixir himself, escapes an attempt on his life, and destroys the elixir and, with it, Killigrew. He is fortuitously restored to his uncle's good graces, marries Rose, and becomes a fisherman, living in "the old house at the foot of the fells."[4]

Ransome's pleasure in the eighteenth-century novelists is obvious, although the book reads far more like Jeffery Farnol's bestselling pastiches of the time than like the genuine article. (Farnol's *The Broad Highway* [1910] is typical.) But what is also clear is Ransome's debt to Wilde (Killigrew is brother to Dorian Gray) and his even greater one to Poe. The ancient home of the Killigrews is very much in Poe's mold:

> Directly before us were more thick woods, and it was not until we were close upon it that I perceived, hidden in these trees, a strange, melancholy-looking old house of stone, covered with dark green ivy, which had grown even to the roof and waved ragged despairing arms from the grey stone copings.
>
> Some of the upper windows were boarded up. . . . The door was studded with iron. . . . The stone steps before it were cracked, and dandelions raised their golden suns from between the cracks. As we rode up, I saw a snake, that had been sunning itself in the last warmth of the day, slip off the step. (*EL,* 28)

Similarly, the fiendish bed with the canopy that slowly descends and then falls to smother its victims, the burning of the hall, and Killigrew's dusty death could all be from Poe's pen.

Ransome's wisest move, perhaps, was to adopt the persona of a young and insecure young man, a romantic, and whether or not this was intended as a self-portrait, it certainly acts as one. The prose, although perhaps a little given to double adjectives, is clear and no more pretentious than one might expect from such a narrator; even the fair Rose has more than a modicum of good sense to balance her adulatory portrait. The plot is unravelled with a keen eye for horrors, as, for example, when the servant Michael (also an elixir drinker) is murdered, and moments later Richard finds not a body, but bones. Many of the scenes are stagey and contrived, but, as the narrator says in the climactic confrontation with Killigrew, he had now to "set an end to this theatrical business" (*EL,* 289–90).

Ransome, in short, produces a serviceable pastiche, well-decorated with philosophical asides on the nature of life, and ending, perhaps prophetically, with a picture of what, at that stage in his life, must have seemed a scarcely attainable idyll. Richard's remarks on his un-

cle (who, in the manner of Stevenson, is presented at the outset as
more or less heartless, despite what the audience can see as considerable provocation), may say something about Ransome's own ideals:
"My uncle died . . . thanking God that his illness had come upon him
at the end of the trout season, instead of at the beginning. He had
the satisfaction of making a fisherman of me, and of fastening a bent
pin on the end of a thread, and seeing his first great-nephew catch a
minnow. I believe he never caught a salmon himself with greater
pride" (*EL,* 311).

Hugh Brogan observes that *The Elixir of Life* "is an odd book, one
about which it would be too easy to be wantonly unkind," describing
it as "such complete tosh as to stifle any regret that Arthur destroyed
so much of his prentice works. The only thing of interest is . . . the
character of the uncle."[5] This judgment seems rather hard. The book
may be melodrama, but it is highly controlled, has scarcely a stum-
ble, and, as melodramas go, has its share of subtlety.

The Elixir of Life, for all its shortcomings, is not the work of an
amateur, and, curiously, it looks forward to Ransome's first genuine
(and lasting) success, *Old Peter's Russian Tales.*

Ransome learned Russian by using children's primers and newspapers. His account, couched in customarily modest terms, of his
method of dealing with the tales may explain the success of his re-
tellings. He began with word-for-word translations, but he discovered
that "direct translation is not the way to tell Russian stories to English children, and for a reason that should have been obvious from
the beginning. The Russian peasant storytellers, telling stories to
each other, could count on a wide range of knowledge that their listeners, no matter how young, shared with them. Young English listeners knew nothing of the world that in Russia listeners and
storytellers alike were able to take for granted. Continual explanation would have been as destructive of the tales as an endless series
of asides" (*A,* 162).

He solved this problem by producing, in *Old Peter's Russian Tales,*
a "frame," which shows clearly his virtues as a writer, once he had
found his voice: precision, unpretentiousness, and a very neat selection of atmospheric details. "In Russia," he writes in an introductory
note, "hardly anybody is too old for fairy stories. . . . My book is not
for the learned, or indeed for grown-up people at all. No people who
really like fairy stories ever grow up altogether." He also linked the
stories with his favorite landscape, with an echo of his old manner:
"This is a book written far away in Russia, for English children who
play in deep lanes with wild roses above them in the high hedges, or
by small singing becks that dance down the grey fells at home. . . .

Under my windows the wavelets of the Volkhov . . . are beating quietly in the dusk."[6]

As Marcus Crouch has observed, "There had been several earlier collections of Russian folk-tales, but none had the freshness, the authentic peasant quality of this, which preserved the waywardness, the alternation of grim and gay, which gives its individual colour to traditional Russian art."[7]

The folk tales are told by a peasant, Old Peter, in a hut in a vast forest, to his two orphan grandchildren, Maroosia and Vanya. The person of Old Peter is seen in the brief introductory passages to each story, and his voice begins most of the tales and then fades away. The pseudo-storyteller is a device used by many recorders of folk-tales, but rarely so successfully as Ransome.

The stories themselves differ, sometimes radically, from the traditions with which most Western children are familiar. Wicked stepmothers, for example, are perhaps outnumbered by domineering and selfish old women. In many of the stories, such as "The Golden Fish" or "The Stolen Turnips," the plot hinges on the selfish, greedy, and unreasonable behavior of the old woman, in contrast with a submissive old man. In "The Stolen Turnips," there is a choice: "This story used to be told in two ways. It was either the tale of an old man who was bothered by a cross old woman, or the tale of an old woman who was bothered by a cross old man" (*OP,* 119). Perhaps needless to say, given Ransome's personal circumstances as a disappointed married man, the tale is told of the forceful and avaricious woman dominating the poor, well-meaning husband.

But perhaps more than in other traditions, the tales deal directly with cruelty and death, pursuit (very effectively in the huge Russian landscape), and, most of all, with the randomness of fate.

With his literary–theoretical leanings, Ransome must have been aware of the structural patterns in his material. (There is no evidence that he was familiar with the Russian formalists.) Several of the tales begin with the central character picking up, or being given, what appears to be a random selection of items (a comb, a ribbon, a bottle of oil). In the second half of the tale, these become magically appropriate as weapons to defeat or delay evil. As we shall see in the "Swallows and Amazons" stories, Ransome sometimes used exactly the same pattern—a slow build-up of acquiring skills, followed by a rather more breathless exploitation of them. His great skill was to make the contrivance seem inevitable (*We Didn't Mean to Go to Sea* is the most striking example).

The Russian tales depart from Ransome's personal morality on the surface in that although the meek generally win, it is commonly chance, not any virtue or hard work, that assures success. The Fool of the World only has to take the advice of a passing old man to become Czar, and that advice was earned by no more than common courtesy. But such courtesy, which breaks down "adult" discriminations between age, sex, class, and even humans and animals, is part of a subconscious code of "decent" behavior. The peasants of the tales have a sinewy toughness and pragmatism that does not desert them, even when they are rewarded with kingdoms.

The amorality (in this sense) of the tales is even more the case with the second collection, *The War of the Birds and the Beasts* (1984).[8] This book was compiled by Hugh Brogan, partly from stories that appeared in periodicals and partly from manuscript. It includes a longer story, "The Soldier and Death," published as a separate volume in 1920. The stories, which take their collective title from a straightforward animal fable, are generally both more cosmic and more sombre than those in *Old Peter*. They also lack the comfortable unifying framework provided by Old Peter himself. If anything, the randomness of fate is more apparent. In the title story, the birds and the beasts fight over trivialities, and the hostilities escalate until the two Czars, the Firebird and the Bear, do battle. The Bear is defeated and blinded, and the injured Firebird is nursed back to health by the peasant–everyman Ivan. Ivan is rewarded with a princess and a palace . . . but what of the Bear?

Similarly, the stories range from the wicked stepmother who is unmasked when her innocent victims rise from the dead, to the blacksmith who has a few moments of sitting on God's throne, seeing the infinite evil of the world. He cannot stand it and tries to climb down: "'No,' God says to him, 'sit you there, and watch and suffer. You, who cannot sit there for one minute, see only what I see. I sit on that throne for ever, age after age, and see all the evil that is done or dreamed, and am patient with it. Let you be patient too'" (*WB*, 83). The blacksmith is sent back to earth.

In "The Soldier and Death," perhaps the strangest of the tales, the soldier hero acquires (by simple kindness) a magic sack, with the aid of which, and with much pragmatic cunning, he first frightens the Devil, and then captures Death itself. He is begged by the old, who cannot die, to release Death—who, thereafter, will have nothing to do with him. The story ends: "Death would not take him. There was no place for him in Paradise and no place for him in hell. For all I know he may be living yet" (*WB*, 104). These tales are in the "trickster" tradition (though with more sombre or ambiguous endings than commonly), which may account for their continuing appeal to children.

Ransome became interested in Russian politics and was appointed correspondent for the *Daily News*. Along with many other projects, further volumes of tales were abandoned. But any reader who has been pursued across the wide world by the thirty-foot-high witch-baby (with her iron teeth), or by Baba Yaga, beating with her pestle and sweeping with her besom, or who has waited in the frozen forest with the poor girl while Frost crackles and laughs among the trees, or who has attended (and this is a piece of naturalistic writing) the christening in the village, will know that *Old Peter's Russian Tales* is a haunting and masterful book, the re-creation not merely of folk-tales, but of a whole time, place, and culture. As Fisher points out, this is the world of Czarist Russia—"not the world of political unrest as Ransome the war correspondent saw it but a world of deep forests, superstition, subsistence lives warmed by robust humour and strong magic."[9] In the 1938 reprint of *Old Peter's Russian Tales,* Ransome provided a characteristically modest introduction: "Fashions change in stories of adventure, but fairy stories (especially those in which there are no fairies or hardly any) live for ever, with a life of their own which depends very little on mere editors (like me) who pass them on."[10]

For the next three years, Ransome's life was as romantic as any writer could wish, although it was made uncomfortable by ill health. He reported the progress of the Russian Revolution, taking the un-popular view that the ultimate success of the Bolsheviks was largely the fault of mismanagement and misunderstanding by the Western governments. He was close to the major figures of the time; he played chess with Lenin and, after his divorce from Ivy in 1924, married Trotsky's secretary, Evgenia Shelepina.

Unfortunately for the general reader, Ransome's account of this period (and, to some extent, Hugh Brogan's as well) goes into the convoluted politics of Russia in such detail that what must have been a fascinating experience is muddied. There are, however, very strik-ing and genuinely romantic moments:

> I went on going to [Trotsky's] office to get such bulletins as his secretary thought fit to dole out, and sometimes to walk with her until we were lucky enough to find a tramcar going towards the centre of the city. Once, I remember, still after these forty years, with a shiver of horror, the tramcar started before she had her foot on the step, and she was dragged, hanging on, along the track, lying on one of the lines so that if her grip had failed she would inevitably have been cut to pieces by the wheels. Those few horrible seconds . . . possibly determined both our lives. (*A,* 231–32)

Ransome's output as a journalist was remarkable. The Brotherton Library at the University of Leeds, for example, has the texts of 564 telegrams, many of them lengthy, sent by Ransome from Russia to the *Daily News* between December 1916 and January 1919. Another forty-four were sent to the *Observer* newspaper between January 1917 and January 1918.

In 1918, he produced a pamphlet, *The Truth about Russia*,[11] but he had already, as Brogan puts it, been written off by the British government as a "dangerous Red." He was investigated by the Foreign Office for his sympathies, and as a result, when he and Evgenia left Russia in 1919, they did not return to England, but for the next five years or so lived in the Baltic states of Estonia and Latvia, which were then independent. Ransome still visited and wrote articles on Russia, and in 1919 published a very vivid and readable account of some of the key events, *Six Weeks in Russia in 1919*.

This book shows two things immediately. The first is how his experience as a correspondent, having to write quickly and succinctly about important factual material, clarified and strengthened his style. The second is how his involvement and commitment gave his writing remarkable force. Both of these tendencies would carry through to his later work. Brogan notes, "Working flat out, Arthur produced his pamphlet in nineteen days, dictating from his loose-leaf notebook to a shorthand typist. . . . His little book may stand in his record as one of his worthiest achievements. It told an important truth at a time when it was badly needed . . . [but] *Six Weeks* is undeniably a work of propaganda."[12]

Six Weeks in Russia in 1919 gets off to a start that is both belligerent and uncertain. "I am well aware that there is material in this book which will be misused by fools both white and red. That is not my fault. My object has been narrowly limited. I have tried by means of a bald record of conversations and things seen, to provide material for those who wish to know what is being done and thought in Moscow at the present time. . . . The book is in no sense of the word propaganda." He also adds the kind of comment with which he prefaced earlier books, but this time it is not a rhetorical gesture: "On reading the manuscript through, I find it quite surprisingly dull. The one thing that I should have liked to transmit through it seems to have slipped away."[13]

In fact, it is a riveting read, despite the fact that Ransome presupposes a knowledge of the situation and speaks always as an insider (another recurrent trait). But although the book is occasionally very dense and even turgid, when dealing with the people and the everyday matters of food or heating, his voice is absolutely clear, and very modern.

> On paying for my room at the beginning of the week I was given a card with the days of the week printed along its edge. This card gave me the right to buy one dinner daily, and when I bought it that day of the week was snipped off so that I could not buy another. The meal consisted of a plate of very good soup, together with a second course of a scrap of meat or fish. . . . One could obtain this meal any time between two and seven. Living hungrily through the morning, at two o'clock I used to experience definite relief in the knowledge that now at any moment I could have my meal. Feeling in this way less hungry I used to postpone it hour by hour, and actually dined about five or six o'clock. (*SWR*, 27–28)

Such anecdotal passages are far more readable than the political ones.

But if no sign of the posing, the pretentious, or the sentimental remains, there is certainly more than a trace of the partisan. He visits an opera from which "the Moscow plutocracy of bald merchants and bejewelled fat wives had gone." He felt that "there were very few people in the theatre who had had anything like a good dinner to digest. But, as for their keenness, I can imagine few audiences to which, from the actor's point of view, it would be better worth while to play." (*SWR*, 61–62)

The prose is engaging (". . . had a fine bumpity ride to the station" [*SWR*, 17]), and he has an eye for the children who are returning to Russia: "I was sorry for the five children who were with us, knowing that a country simultaneously suffering war, blockade and revolution is not a good place for childhood. But they had caught the mood of their parents, revolutionaries going home to their revolution, and trotted excitedly up and down the carriage or anchored themselves momentarily, first on one person's knee and then another's" (*SWR*, 5).

This book is undoubtedly uneven, and its political partiality is of a piece with the unmistakably democratic tone of his later children's books. But its intensity and vitality, and its stubbornness in concentrating on the mundane positives of the Russian Revolution rather than on the corruptions and massacres, is, even now, a rather startling corrective; the book deserves to be reprinted, with good footnotes by a reliable historian.

One is left with a feeling of honesty ("I spent the whole of my time in ceaseless investigation . . . until at the end of a month I was so tired (besides being permanently hungry) that I began to fear rather than to seek new experiences and impressions" [*SWR*, 126]), and a certain pride in his achievement. However, when he takes his leave of Lenin, to whom he was undoubtedly sympathetic, the tone is uncomfortably reminiscent of Gulliver taking his leave of the Master of the Houyhnhnms in Book Four of Swift's *Gulliver's Travels*. In *Six Weeks in Russia* Ransome writes: "I said I should be very sorry to think that this was my last visit to the country which I love only second to my own. He laughed, and paid me the compliment of saying that 'although English,' I had more or less succeeded in understanding what they were at, and that he should be pleased to see me again" (*SWR*, 151). Swift, mocking the naivety and "slave mentality" of Gulliver, has him write: "[My master] concluded that for his own part he could have been content to keep me in his service . . . because he found I had cured myself of some bad habits and dispositions, by endeavouring, as far as my inferior nature was capable, to imitate the Houyhnhnms. . . . I told him I would . . . [celebrate] the praises of the renowned Houyhnhnms, and [propose] their virtues to the imitation of mankind."[14]

To a generation used to assuming that Bolshevism was an evil movement, it may seem a long and naive step for Ransome from his apolitical local democratic outlook to that of "Red" sympathiser. Even Brogan clearly implies that Ransome was used by the Russian politicians and that his point of view was partial. (There is something of a parallel here with Wordsworth's response to the French Revolution.) In a period full of atrocities, Ransome seems to have suppressed comment on the atrocities committed by the side he favored. To some extent this was a corrective to the generally biased reporting of the situation; but to a larger extent it was characteristic of his strong enthusiasms. Ransome seems to have espoused causes much as he espoused people, places, and skills, and all of these brought on a certain tunnel vision. What he saw (and what he chose to see) was, however, described with such shrewdness and clarity that a reader may well wish that the pictures he presents were more rounded, in both fact and fiction.

Six Weeks in Russia was not quite his last word on the subject. His less successful *The Crisis in Russia* was published in 1921,[15] and he contributed an article on Russia to the *Encyclopaedia Brittanica* in 1926. But his attention had now turned to an altogether more peaceful occupation, one that was to color his writing for the rest of his life: sailing.

On 20 August 1922, Ransome, with Evgenia and one Captain Sehmel (to whom Ransome always referred as the "Ancient Mariner" and
who "also served as the model for Peter Duck" [*A,* 306]) set sail in the
Baltic in Ransome's new boat, *Racundra.* Ransome kept a detailed
log of the voyage, and began to work the material into a book three
weeks after their return. His intention was to produce a book that
was both a sailing book and a travel book—as well as being, as Brogan puts it, a love story.[16]

To the nonsailor, *Racundra's First Cruise* is a curious volume; it is
a specialist work, full of small details of what was a relatively uneventful voyage and many pages of the minutiae of sailing and rig-
ging and navigating, which are largely incomprehensible to the
layperson. That this is a book for the initiated is signalled by the
opening sentence: "Houses are but badly built boats so firmly
aground that you cannot think of moving them."[17]

Racundra was Ransome's attempt to build the perfect boat. The
first chapter is a restrained account of how the boat was conceived,
built, and finally taken away from the boatbuilders, unfinished. As
he remarked wryly, "Fools build and wise men buy" (*RFC,* 15). This
and his subsequent experiences with tardy boatbuilders surfaced
many years later in an episode in the Lake District novel *The Picts
and the Martyrs.* In that book, the children visit the boatyard to see
if their new dinghy is ready. It isn't, and "the old boatbuilder did not
even think he needed to say he was sorry." Nancy Blackett, captain
of the *Amazon,* invokes her Uncle Jim, Ransome's alter ego: "'Uncle
Jim's quite right. You know what he said?' 'Nay, I don't.' 'He said you
were bound to be late with her because the only boatbuilder who ever
finished a boat on time was Noah, and he only did it because he knew
he'd be drowned if he didn't.' 'He's one for joking, is Mr. Turner,' said
the old man."[18]

Ransome leavened the account of sailing of *Racundra* with encounters ashore, and possibly because they are "padding" and not focussed
on his dominant interest of the time, some of these are in his worst
manner—pseudo-symbolic, inconsequential, and rather pretentious.
(An example is chapter 16, "The Ship and the Man," first published
in the *Manchester Guardian* in 1922).

However, as always, when Ransome is describing things that he
admires and that are admirably odd, his prose becomes pristine. For
example, at Heltermaa, on the Island of Dago, he describes a
steamer, the *Toledo,* aground on a shoal in the Baltic. After the war,
she had been taken over by a salvage company, and one Captain
Konga was living aboard, waiting until the water level rose high
enough to float her off. Konga, living a timeless existence, had waited

two years. Ransome describes his cabin—a description that was echoed many years later in the cabins of the "Speedy" in *Secret Water* and of the eelman in *The Big Six:*

> I have seen many cabins, but none quite like that hutch in which the captain of the *Toledo* had his comfortable being. It was built of baulks of wood set up on end between the iron decks. It was six feet six inches high, long and broad. That size, Captain Konga explained, he had found by experiment to be the most convenient. Sitting on his bunk, he could put wood on the stove in the corner, light his reading-lamp, take a book from the opposite shelf, eggs or bacon from his store-cupboard, reach down his saucepan or frying-pan from the hooks on the wall. . . . From any place in it he could reach every other place, and that, he said, was the most labour-saving kind of house. (*RFC*, 120–21)

This episode is one of several reported not from the first cruise of *Racundra,* but from earlier potterings on the Baltic, notably with his previous boat, *Kittiwake.* One of the curious features of *Racundra's First Cruise* is that is seems almost a sequel, or a book written for people intimately acquainted not just with sailing, but with Ransome's life. Old friends, in the form of boats as well as people, continually crop up, scarcely introduced. *Kittiwake* and *Slug* are referred to as though we knew them well.

This habit, together with the feeling that a "ghost" book is being raided to bulk out the not very exciting voyage of *Racundra,* gives the book its rather rarefied air, with a remarkable lack of narrative thrust or structural cohesion. However, what seems to be a failing in *Racundra's First Cruise* was elevated into an art in the children's books, especially *Swallowdale. Racundra's First Cruise* represents the triumph of the specialist occupation over the demands of narrative, *Swallowdale* the blending of the two. In the earlier book, the interest has to be sustained by what would for the nonspecialist normally be background material; in *Swallowdale,* the background material has a broader appeal.

One of the best features of *Racundra's First Cruise* is the relationship between the ship and her master. The other characters (the "Cook" and the "Ancient Mariner") scarcely exist. As a sample, here is the passage between Pakerort and Reval, where there is a vivid description of "careering through steep seas in a pitch-dark night with no sidelights and a binnacle lamp that would not burn." Far from being "misery," Ransome had "the definite impression that *Racundra* was enjoying it also in her fashion. I found myself, who do not sing in happier moments, yelling 'Spanish Ladies' and 'Summer is icumen in' and 'John Peel' at the top of my voice." Then Evgenia makes her appearance:

> The Cook struggled up the companion way with a sandwich. She asked, with real inquiry, "Are we going to be drowned before morning?"
> I leaned forward from the steering-well and shouted, "Why?"
> "Because I have two thermos flasks full of hot coffee. If we are, we may as well drink them both. If not, I'll keep one till tomorrow."
> . . . The more we ate the better things seemed. . . . Douses of spray merely made it seem worth while to have put on oilskins . . . The Cook, who had been doing her work as calmly as *Racundra,* and like *Racundra* was enjoying it, fell asleep in the middle of a laugh. She was tired out, and when the next big splash woke her, I sent her below to lie down. (*RFC,* 47–48)

This extract is one of many that could be cited to show how well Ransome later quarried his experiences for the "Swallows and Amazons" books. The mention of the sea shanty "Spanish Ladies", which the children sing in several of the books, is an example, while the lack of riding lights provides one of the most exciting episodes in *We Didn't Mean to Go to Sea.* It is illuminating to compare the voyage to Reval with the experience of the children on the "North Sea." In this scene, John is sailing the *Goblin* at night, with a strong following wind.

> [John] settled himself to his steering and to keeping a look out at the same time.
> With the doors of the cabin closed there was no light in the cockpit, except a feeble glimmer where the little candle-lamp, hidden from outside, threw a pale yellow glow over the compass card inside the window. . . .
> So . . . and back. . . . So . . . and back. . . . Lean and sway with this triumphant motion. Good little ship. . . . He put a hand over the edge of the coaming and patted the damp deck in the darkness. . . .
> Whatever happened, he simply must not go to sleep. If only he could sing it would be easier to keep awake. But he could not sing because of waking Susan.
> Suddenly he started. A sail was clapping like thunder. The wind was blowing not from behind him, but into his face.

ALL BUT O.B.

The tiller was kicking this way and that and the *Goblin* was plunging up and down like a mad thing.[19]

Later on, Susan, trying to keep him awake, has to pinch him (*WDM* 206). Compare that fictional episode with the facts. Back on the real Baltic, Ransome is at the tiller:

> So we went on, hour after hour, until I too fell asleep.
> I suppose everybody who has spent long hours at the tiller of a little boat has done the same. But, I admit, I was startled the first time I woke to find myself in the steering-well of *Racundra* holding a kicking tiller, with the dark in my eyes and a great wind in my face. The next time it happened, I said to myself "Done it again!" and began pinching myself as hard as I could, in muscles, in any places that seemed to hurt, in the effort to keep awake. It was no use. (*RFC*, 48)

Cruising in *Racundra,* then, not only resulted in Ransome's first "real" book but also marked a transition point, between his travels as a reporter and his future literary career. He was offered work by Ted Scott of the *Manchester Guardian* (later the *Guardian*). Ransome wrote to his mother: "My job is to include a fortnightly or possibly weekly article on the fishing in the whole district north of Manchester. . . . I think it will mean a lot of open air in pursuit of things that I am interested in anyway, it will mean a very jolly life in itself."[20] His divorce from Ivy came through, and he and Evgenia were married at Reval.

Late in 1924, leaving *Racundra* in the hands of the "Ancient Mariner," he and Evgenia moved back to England. The following year, they bought a small cottage in the Lake District, "Low Ludderburn." It had water from a Roman well, a large barn that Ransome converted into a workroom, an orchard, and one and three-quarters acres with wonderful views: in short, it was idyllic. It cost £550, and the *Manchester Guardian* was paying Ransome £300 per year plus "piece rates."

The move marked the end of his involvement in politics. His work on the *Manchester Guardian* involved him with people whose attitudes were on the left of the political spectrum, but that association was as far as his participation went. His feelings were summed up neatly in this quotation, broadcast in a BBC program:

> I remember when I was in Russia, the *Daily News* sent me some tobacco. . . . At the first puff, I was back at home drinking beer with Lascelles Abercrombie in the "Hark to Melody"

by Haverthwaite. . . . It was no good. The Russian revolution
had failed utterly in altering me personally, and I vowed
that once I got a little peace and quiet and had got my sketch
of the development of the revolution written, I would write
"finis" and fetch politics a good boost with the boot in the
latter parts and return with no regrets whatever to pen, to-
bacco, fishing, and the lake country.[21]

Ransome had returned to his roots, and although both the worlds
of journalism and travel still had some claims to make on him, it
would not be long before his third, and most famous, literary career
began.

3

Fishing, Sailing, and "Swallows and Amazons"

Ironically, the first fruits of Ransome's new life had to do neither with the Lake District nor with the sailing and fishing that absorbed him. The *Manchester Guardian* was still sending him abroad (although he was increasingly reluctant to go), and over Christmas 1926 he found himself in China.

The Chinese Puzzle (1927) was published with a foreword by David Lloyd George (Prime Minister of Great Britain until 1922). According to Hugh Brogan, the trip "had fallen totally flat",[1] a dismissal that suggests that its only real value was the material it provided for the children's book *Missee Lee*. Brogan's comment is not quite fair, for even more than Ransome's books on Russia, *The Chinese Puzzle* blends vivid reporting and personal involvement.

Typically, he plunges straight into a complicated and detailed analysis of the British presence in China. Broadly speaking, he describes how the British had put troops rather than police into their foreign "concessions"—areas of cities or ports ceded to foreign countries. In the face of the Chinese Revolution going on around them, the British had "for military necessity" moved their troops into Chinese territory outside the concessions.

Ransome's views come over very clearly, and his analyses are forceful and typical. He was not surprised that the Chinese thought that the British were aggressors. Writing of Mrs Sun Yat-sen (who was educated at Wesleyan College, Galveston) and the government at Hankow (whose language was English, as all but one of them had been educated in England or America), he points out: "Nor should we be in any way surprised at finding that the leaders of Chinese nationalism are the men who have been taught by the West. . . . We should resent the spectacle of forty foreign ships of war anchored in the Thames without invitation from ourselves, or that sandbags and barbed wire were put up by the inhabitants of the Chinese quarter in an English city. We ought to be rather flattered than surprised that Western-educated Chinese have learnt something of this proud intolerance from ourselves."[2]

He was unimpressed by what he saw to be selfish financial motives on the part of the Western powers; and he pointed out that Chinese communism was not comparable with Russian: "Communism at this point of Chinese history is a wholly irrelevant slogan. The China in which that slogan might have real meaning does not yet exist, and consequently Chinese Communists . . . are sufficiently like Communists to get their heads cut off, but that is all. . . . It is an accident that a number of the young Chinese revolutionaries call themselves Communists, though it is not an accident that . . . foreign businessmen in China seize upon this name to justify as 'anti-Communism' actions and policies which have a much more personal motive" (*CP*, 38–39).

For example, the "revolutionary" change in the law of inheritance to the Western idea ("inheritance . . . in the direct line only, unless a man draws up a specific will to dispose of his property") was entirely capitalist. The old idea, that "when a man died all his relations shared in his inheritance" was a far more "communist" principle (*CP*, 38).

The prose is sharp and convincing, and the attitude one of liberal anticapitalism, a point worth remembering when we come across the nostalgia of his later work. But, as before, one might not expect his political views to be popular. A reader who took political history from Ransome might well be convinced that in both Russia and China the attitude of the West played a large part in fostering the communist states we see today. He emphasizes, prophetically, Russia's continual feeling of threat from the West, and notes, "Poland is continually waving a sword, a little too heavy for that little country to carry alone, on Russia's Western frontiers" (*CP*, 77). Even more than before, Ransome seems devoted to redressing the balance of reportage as much as espousing a cause.

But among the shrewd political observations are very vivid passages describing the Chinese landscape and Chinese customs. His stay in Hankow (Wuhan) coincided with the Chinese New Year, and the Chinese themselves, "with a certain triumphal air," paraded through the "once sacred" streets of the concessions.

A crowd of men and boys with paper lanterns, gay by day and still gayer at night, precede a dragon borne aloft on poles by twenty or thirty men at regular intervals along its snake-like length. It has a huge carved head painted red, blue, yellow, and white, with loose, goggling, swaying eyes. Its body is a long tube enclosing at intervals barrel-shaped lanterns. It ends in a carved tail, desperately waggled by a skilful bearer. Immediately before it marches a juggler, swinging two lanterns, at the ends of ropes, round and round and in and out like Indian clubs, twirling and dancing as he goes. The whole procession is surrounded by gong-beaters, cymbal-bangers, rattlers of split bamboo sticks, and frenzied spendthrifts of fire-crackers. (*CP,* 49)

Fourteen years later, these descriptions were to add authenticity to his most exotic children's book, *Missee Lee.* Towards the end of that book, the little dragon made up of the "Swallows" and the "Amazons" dances through the festival. (Roger swings the lantern; the head is carried by Uncle Jim and the tail by Titty.)

Ransome's work for the *Manchester Guardian,* writing essays on fishing, also bore fruit. *Rod and Line,* containing fifty articles reprinted from the newspaper, was originally published in 1929 by Jonathan Cape; the original edition also included a long essay on the Russian fisherman Sergei Aksakov. That essay, which Brogan describes as "large chunks of translation surrounded by stretches of commentary,"[3] was dropped from the Oxford University Press reprint of *Rod and Line* in 1980, although Ransome mentions Aksakov while discussing his library of fishing books in *Mainly about Fishing* (1959): "I think of the chapters on fishing, chapters from which the very essence of angling pleasure seems to distil like the mist rising on a summer's morning from a placid river, that were written by a Russian, Sergei Aksakov . . . who said that trout-fishing was 'too restless' and preferred to watch his float. No man has written as well as he of the ecstasy felt by a boy as he comes to the river and of the calm happiness felt by an old man fishing in the evening of his life the waters he knew as a boy."[4] (In that book's list of "books by the same author," *Rod and Line* appears as *Rod and Line: with Aksakov on Fishing.*)

Rod and Line is an amiable collection, very little scarred by Ransome's earlier florid style. Broadly, there are three kinds of articles: first, erudite reviews of fishing literature, such as "North Country Fishing Ninety Years Ago," which introduces us to Stephen Oliver's

Recollections of Fly-Fishing (1834) (Oliver reappears in *Mainly about Fishing* in "The Travelling Companion"); second, pieces characterized by a combination of dry wit and wry innocence, such as "Fishing Inns," "On Tackle Shops," and "Fishing in Books and Fishing in Fact"; and third, technical pieces that demonstrate Ransome's dedication and range of knowledge, such as "The Dry-fly Strike," "The Winged Ant," and "Left-handed Winding."

The second category makes this book accessible to the layman. In "A Day of Small Things," Ransome fishes the lower reaches of his favorite river, and ends with a typical pastoral:

> Just then two rabbits came from their burrows in the sandy opposite bank, and sat motionless for half an hour, watching me. At the end of that time one of them scratched his neck with his hind-leg. That showed a profound increase in confidence and thereafter, until I got up to pack my things and go, the rabbits fed, pausing only when I lifted my rod to cast or to bring a fish to bank. A huge flock of rooks passed over. Peewits called. Hidden in the deep bank of the river I was . . . isolated from the world except for the two rabbits, the opposite bank, twenty yards of brown stream and the blue sky overhead.[5]

Ransome is not, however, above irritating (however innocently) the mere mortals among us—especially those who live in these overfished and polluted days. He goes on, apparently without exaggeration or irony, "Nor did I catch much. Another half-pound perch, a little one put back, and three more eels at decent intervals punctuated the afternoon. Four little jack [i.e., pike], four small eels and a brace of perch" (*RL,* 120). This sounds suspiciously like the writers with whom he has fun in "Fishing in Books and Fishing in Fact," where, as he says, "In books the fish and the weather know their parts" (*RL,* 13). But he can also laugh at himself: "Finally, after fishing till dusk, you set off home. On the way, you take a cast, just for luck, in a place where you missed a good one, and get caught up in a tree behind you. You break your cast, strain the middle joint of your rod in taking it to pieces . . . and in taking off your waders learn that they have been torn by a bramble" (*RL,* 15–16).

One refreshing thing about the book is that its pontifications no longer have the sound of a young man trying to be old. By staying within the bounds of what he knows and what he has learned to judge from experience, his views have gained authority. He is now, as Richard Jefferies was in his best books, drawing upon his "insider's" knowledge, and, like Jefferies, writing with an economy born of years of journalism. For example, he thinks that serving luncheon at midday "betrays a bad fishing inn. . . . In a good fishing inn they have forgotten how to make luncheons, for all their guests grab sandwiches, rush out immediately after breakfast and come back hungry for dinner with the sandwiches still in their pockets because they have never had time to eat them. An inn that expects its guests to come in for luncheon in the middle of the day is an inn with a bad conscience, which knows that its water is not worth fishing (*RL*, 89).

In 1929, Ransome published two short stories in the *Pall Mall Magazine:* "Two Shorts and a Long" (May, vol. 5, no. 1) and "The Unofficial Side" (September, vol. 5, no. 5).[6] They are both sea stories for adults, and might well have been by W. W. Jacobs, Saki, or Kipling. But they are highly significant in Ransome's development, both symbolically and stylistically. With journalism, revolution, and an unsuccessful marriage behind him, Ransome was finding his own voice.

The first, "Two Shorts and a Long" (the morse code signal for "you are standing into danger") begins with a scene that readers of Ransome will recognize, one that is echoed in *We Didn't Mean to Go to Sea:*

> The water was like oil, as much as you could see of it from the yacht. There was nothing else to be seen, except the lower parts of the rigging, in the thick blanket of fog that surrounded Hurst and I, in oilskins in the little cockpit, drinking hot tea that Hurst, my paid hand, had brewed on the stove in the cabin. We had run out of the fairway and anchored in four fathom of water but, even so, one of us had to be on deck ready with the foghorn when necessary and, as we were not too sure of our position, I had not been able to settle down below. (*CN*, 80)

The simple story that Hurst tells, about the young owner of a yacht cruising in the Baltic who falls in love and ignores his deckhand's warning, is romantic enough, but it is mediated through a pair of unromantic eyes. The girl turns out to be a good sailor, not some laughing nymph.

The second story is more enigmatic, and the only instance of Ransome using his Russian experience in fiction. It is not only symbolic of Ransome's political attitudes, but a resolution of them. Hurst, alias Ransome, is in Petrograd. By a combination of accidents, he steals a yacht in order to help an escapee from the Communists. Running to Estonia, he also picks up a Communist escapee. He deposits both men in suitable places and sinks the yacht before returning to his job as deckhand on a private yacht. Hurst is apolitical; if anything, he prefers the Communist passenger, but his justice is that both are left to their own devices—and any trace of his own involvement must be completely wiped out. Only then can Hurst/Ransome return to the simple professional world of sailing. This is, of course, politically and philosophically at best naive, and at worst deliberately inward-looking. But although it may seem like an abnegation and an escape, it can also be seen as a deliberate return to a true path. The parallel with Wordsworth (both in biographical fact and in the self-justification of *The Prelude*) breaks down; Ransome made a positive break with his political past. Shortly after Hurst has walked through Petrograd, "being distracted by looking at the red flags and the bullet marks in the houses and other trophies of the Revolution" (*CN*, 94), Ransome takes him to sea, and does not neglect the technical details of sailing: "Then, as quiet as I could, I hoisted the mainsail, belaying peak halyards while I seated on the throat, same's you do yourself, sir, when you're alone. I didn't dare haul too hard on the peak" (*CN*, 98). The story is a transition from Ransome's old world to the new.

Interesting as these books and stories were, they were resolutions rather than new beginnings. Ransome was enjoying himself in the Lake District, and in 1928 the famous catalyst to his talent was provided. Dora Collingwood had married Ernest Altounyan and moved to Aleppo in Syria. In April 1928 they returned to the Lake District with their five children: Taqui, Susan, Mavis (who was nicknamed "Titty"), Roger, and Brigit. Ransome and Ernest bought the children two sailing dinghies, *Swallow* and *Mavis,* and Ransome helped to teach them to sail.

At the same time the *Manchester Guardian* offered him a large salary to become their Berlin correspondent, with a prospect of becoming their literary editor in due course. Happy and not wishing to go back to travel and political journalism, Ransome resigned, and shortly after began the first of his children's books, *Swallows and Amazons*. It was inspired by and dedicated to the Altounyan children, although the eldest girl, Taqui, was changed into the fictional John for the sake of balance. Ransome was so taken with the book that he recalled in his *Autobiography* that every evening he would bring the manuscript from his workroom "so that I could reach out and lay my hand on it in the dark beside my bed" (*A*, 331).

The first two books, *Swallows and Amazons* and *Swallowdale,* sold slowly, but the success of *Peter Duck* (written partly in the Altounyan's house in Aleppo) assured Ransome's future. From then on, a book was added to the series every year or every other year until *The Picts and the Martyrs* in 1943 and *Great Northern?* in 1947.

Swallows and Amazons was at first issued without illustrations. Eleanor Graham, who ran the children's room at a famous bookshop, "Bumpus," describes an encounter with Ransome:

> One day, Ransome himself came up to the Children's Room. I saw him on the step, and watched as he sidled round the walls, not looking in my direction—but making sure I was still there. He wanted to know at first hand how it was doing, but hated to ask. I knew that, and told him at once that I liked it, and that it had made a good start. He spotted a reserve in my mind, and I was obliged to go further. I told him I was sorry there were no pictures—even just to break up the long stretches of text. He nodded. Yes, he understood that ... but pictures? ... A grumbly sort of pause.... They'd take a long time to do. I wondered if he really had any idea of illustrating it himself? (Attractive illustrations, if possible by a known artist, were almost vital to a children's book's success.) I did not ask the question, but he followed me, and mumbled crossly, "An artist would be sure to get everything wrong." That was evidently more than he could bear. *"Good mind to do them myself,"* he muttered.
> Could he, I wondered? But I only spoke of the time it would take him. He nodded, yes, that was just the trouble. He rambled off, with no goodbye.[7]

Ransome subsequently illustrated *Swallows and Amazons* (and all the other books) in inimitable style. As Crouch observes, the drawings "were superficially peculiar, for he had little technique in draughtsmanship. The queer drawings had one overwhelming advantage over other artist's [*sic*] work; they illustrated just those points on which elucidation was needed. The pictures were in fact working drawings which showed how the numerous technical problems in the stories were worked out."[8] The drawings, sometimes made from posed photographs, were a matter of some pride for Ransome. Like Tenniel's illustrations for the "Alice" books, or Shepard's for *The Wind in the Willows,* they have become an integral part of the texts.

Ransome became famous and financially secure. He was able to live where he wished (he and Evgenia moved frequently), and to indulge his passion for sailing and fishing. He had built for him, or bought, a succession of boats, two of which, *Peter Duck* and *Nancy Blackett,* were named after characters in his books. He formed many friendships with children who shared his interests, and all accounts suggest that he was well liked, not least because of his childlike-ness.

THE START OF THE VOYAGE

He was able to distill his experiences and pleasures—and friends—
into his books; he was, as he said, able to indulge the pleasure of his
heart.

He wrote very little apart from the "Swallows and Amazons" books
between 1930 and 1947, whereas from 1948 onward he provided erudite and enthusiastic introductions to several of publisher Rupert
Hart-Davis's "Mariners Library," in which *Racundra's First Cruise*
was included in 1958.

By the 1950s Ransome had an international reputation and both
civil and academic honors. He was even a favourite of royalty: "Both
Princess Elizabeth and her sister have an inbred love of boats and
the sea, and . . . at Windsor castle, have often repeated, at least in
imagination, some of the daring exploits of the Swallows and the
Amazons."[9] His younger self would also have been pleased, no doubt,
by Hugh Shelley, who kept a bookshop in Littlehampton and described him in his late sixties "blowing in . . . in full sail under a
voluminous oilskin, a nautical Chesterton."[10] But his health was not
good, and after a stormy voyage when he was seventy, in his yacht
Lottie Blossom to Cherbourg, he finally gave up the sea in 1954.

If Ransome's judgment about boats was erratic (in 1946 he sold
Peter Duck and then bought her back again, at a loss),[11] his judgment
about where to live was even more so. He and Evgenia constantly
moved, and even Hugh Brogan, Ransome's faithful biographer, seems
to lose patience with his subject: "Being the Ransomes, they moved
back to the Lake District, presumably because the climate suited
Genia so little; sold [the yacht] *Peter Duck* . . . because they both en-
joyed sailing, and sea air was so good for Arthur; and took on not just
Lowick Hall . . . a large house, but the farm that went with it, although Arthur was a semi-invalid and Genia had never been able to
bear servants of any kind."[12]

Ransome contributed *Fishing,* a garrulous pamphlet on books
about fishing to the National Book League's "Readers Guides," showing his immense erudition. Typically he drew to a close with the
words, "But I am rattling on too long."[13] This pamphlet was expanded
and quarried for Ransome's last book. Like *Racundra's First Cruise,
Mainly about Fishing* (1959) is an uncompromising book by an expert
for experts. It begins with a declaration of intent—"Much of this
book, is concerned with the extraordinary relationship between the
fly-fisher and the salmon" (*MF,* xi)—but the book ranges more widely
than that. "It is thirty years," Ransome goes on, "since I last put together a fishing book and I have taken the risk of including with the
chapters on that major mystery some things of quite another kind.
Thirty years is a long time and, after all, one stuffs a lot of odds and

ends into one's dubbing box or bag on the off chance that sooner or later one will be glad not to have thrown them away" (*MF,* iv).

The tone is very similar to that of *Rod and Line,* as the close and expert gaze of the true addict rests on matters of fly-tying, which are virtually inpenetrable to the layman. But a relaxed and slightly scholarly air equally pervades his excursions into fishing diaries, with many erudite examples, and his critique of Izaak Walton's texts.

For the fishing diaries, he draws upon Nathaniel Hawthorne, who stayed at the "Swan" in Newby Bridge in the Lake District in 1855, on Dorothy Wordsworth, on Kilvert, and on lesser mortals. He throws in not only reflections on modern life ("How much better were things then [in Wordsworth's day] than now when news is shouted out of a machine and millions of us are kept waiting hour by hour upon events we can do nothing to change" [*MF,* 3]), but also ironic comments—for example, that fishing diaries become "useful for checking the elasticity of fish. It is a scientific fact that a fish for some hours after it has been taken from the water loses weight. It is a fact of human psychology that thereafter the fish makes up what he has lost and begins to expand. . . . Give a fish a chance and he will grow" (*MF,* 5–6). The heathen may joke about this observation, but the true fisherman knows that accuracy and truth are the only essentials.

The general reader may enjoy "The Travelling Companion" (the jointed fishing rod) or "Why Dress Flies," but "Salmon Chew Gum: The Story of the Elver-Fly" is purely for the addict. By a process of deduction, Ransome works out why salmon, which do not feed on their upstream passage, actually rise to flies. This article involves feathers from the Vulturine Guineafowl, identified by his friend Major Myles North (who supplied the story, as we shall see, for *Great Northern?*). So thorough is the scientist–fisherman that a short chapter is devoted entirely to the said Vulturine Guineafowl, complete with colored plate.

Ransome continues this theme in "Doubts about the Concertina Theory" (that you use different flies on different days), while "Natural Selection and the Salmon Fly" puts forward a serious, even scholarly theory of why certain flies are successful and where we should look for further developments.

Much of the book is given to antiquarian pieces, such as "A Cromwellian Trooper's Dubbing Bag," or a look at an unpublished "North Country Notebook" that runs from 1878 to 1894. Then there is "An Eighteenth-Century Poacher," which is a description of an anonymous book of 1786, *The North Country Angler; or the Art of Angling; as practiced in the northern counties of England;* "The Shoemaker of St Boswell's," an exploration of John Younger's *River Angling for Salmon and Trout* (1840); and "Liverpool Banker," an examination of

George Bainbridge's *The Fly-Fishers Guide,* of similar vintage. Some of these pieces are simultaneously anecdotal and technical; others, grouped as "Some Victorian Fly-Dressers" with samples of their work, include the technical details of flies mentioned in the books. His reflections on "A Library of Fishing Books" makes a point on writing that could apply to all of Ransome's books, for young and old: "Writing is a form of living. Readers, overhearing, as it were, an author muttering to himself, share his experience in so far as they are capable, but, being different from him, modify it into an experience of their own. It is obvious that reader and author share in a book's success and that the character of that success depends on both of them" (*MF,* 137; also in *Fishing,* 8–9).

The last chapter of *Mainly about Fishing* is, appropriately enough, a discussion of Isaac Walton, who published "his quiet and peaceful little book" into the "brutal and contentious world" of 1653. Ransome, by paying tribute to the greatest of a series of practical, skilled outdoor men, seems to be trying to define himself: "His book is a new kind of portrait and a new kind of pastoral, but Walton never forgot that it was also to be a practical treatise, 'not unworthy the perusal of most anglers'" (*MF,* 149).

He ends on a slightly apocryphal note, and one that again shows that, with the exception of the "Swallows and Amazons" series, he was never really in full control of the cadences of his writing: "And to-day? We are an audience in some ways not unlike that for which Walton wrote. We, too, live in times of war and of ideological struggle, when civilisation, perhaps the world itself, seems threatened with its end, and that calm book of innocent happiness, that pure, limpid prose of his, addressed in days of strife to all who hate contention, is like a lark singing in the blue sky, high over no-man's-land, above the acrid smoke and the thunder of guns" (*MF,* 151).

One other start to a book has been recently rediscovered. In 1931, Ransome wrote to a friend that he had an idea for a book, which came to be called *The River Comes First.* It was a celebration of professionalism in fishing and gamekeeping, centering on a single river—very much the distillation of everything he had implied in his other books about professionalism and love of place. Parts were drafted as first person narrative (one such episode, "The Cloudburst," has been recently reprinted);[14] four chapters were rewritten in the third person.

What survives shows Ransome at his best. As we have noted before, he was writing in a tradition of which Richard Jefferies was a major exponent, and there are several similarities in their literary lives. Jefferies, who also had a rural boyhood, was a sportsman and naturalist. His early books were excruciating novels (*Restless Human Hearts* is a characteristic title); he then turned to writing articles about agriculture and nature, where he found his true voice. He produced one very curious mixture of children's book, mystical treatise, melodrama, and animal fable, *Wood Magic* (1881), and one masterpiece *about* childhood that has become a classic for children, *Bevis* (1882). (We shall look at this book in more detail when considering *Swallows and Amazons;* it is included in a list that Ransome himself compiled for children.)[15] Jefferies's best nonfiction (or semifiction) was *The Gamekeeper at Home* (1878), where he was using material that he knew and loved; he was an expert's expert. With *The River Comes First,* Ransome was reaching the same ground.

The River Comes First begins by re-creating just the rural scholar–fisherman that Ransome so admired and whom he had documented so well in *Mainly about Fishing.* In some ways, *The River Comes First* is a fictionalized distillation of that book, as well as possibly being, as Brogan suggests, a metaphor for Ransome's own life.[16]

The central character is Tom Staunton, who was based on Tom Stainton, the keeper of Ransome's favorite river, the Bela. After a brief time away, Tom returns to his river, to become, as it were, an ultimate expert. The book also conveys much of the nostalgia, the sense of loss for better, purer times, that runs, mutedly, throughout Ransome's books for children. It is almost as though the false nostalgia that he experienced in "Bohemia" had finally found a genuine expression. *The River Comes First* shows, sadly, how far Ransome might have gone.

In the first scene of the book, we are taken into Canon John William's village school and shown, at once, Ransome's delight in the eccentric:

> During all but the coldest months of the year there was no glass in [one of the windows], and that was for a very good reason. The old vicar was proud of his roses and pansies and waged unceasing war on rabbits. His high desk at the back of the schoolroom was on a raised platform, and on top of the desk was a gun rest with a double barrelled gun on it. The boys, looking up from their desks below, could see the grey shining muzzle sticking out . . . till there was a deafening bang, the schoolroom would be filled with smoke (there was no smokeless powder in those days) and the two boys at the end of the bench nearest the window would leap out, race down the lawn and bring in the rabbit. (*CN,* 27)

The long episode that follows, in which schoolmaster and schoolboy catch salmon together, is as intricate and exciting as similar scenes in Ransome's mature children's books, notably *The Big Six.*

But whether, as Brogan suggests, because of Evgenia's discouragement, or for some other reason, *The River Comes First* was not completed, and Ransome wrote no more fiction. As his health deteriorated he could be irascible about old and new grievances. Rather like the aging Wordsworth, who fulminated about railways in the Lake District, "the question of caravan sites in the Lake District . . . became something which could be guaranteed to provoke a burst of rage."[17] Perhaps saddest of all, he turned against the Altounyans. He suppressed the original dedication to *Swallows and Amazons* and ignored them in his prefatory note to the later editions, and his references to them in the *Autobiography* are little short of insulting.

Yet his friends describe him as a likable, erudite, and entertaining old man, living in a household ruled by the robust Evgenia.

After a long illness, he died 3 June 1967 and was buried in the isolated graveyard at Rusland, in a part of the Lake District that he particularly liked. Evgenia outlived him by eight years, and died on the day that she was to move, yet again, from Oxfordshire to Girton, near Cambridge. She too is buried at Rusland.

4

Introducing the "Swallows
and Amazons" Series

With over a million words written about the Walker children who sail
in the dinghy *Swallow* (and who are thus known as the "Swallows")
and their friends, it might be useful for the reader coming to Ransome for the first time to have an outline of the books. Aficionados
may want to pass immediately to the more detailed analyses in chapters 5–8, but for the uninitiated, this chapter will discuss what the
books are about and who the characters are who move through them.

Let us begin with the characters, admittedly doing them (and Ransome) a great injustice by introducing them in crude thumbnail
sketches. Three families of children are (primarily) involved: the
Walkers (Swallows), the Blacketts (Amazons)—both named after
their boats—and the Callums (the D.'s), who are named from their
first initials.

The first and most important family in the books is the Walkers,
who, on their holidays, usually sail in the borrowed dinghy "Swallow." (It is not clear why, given his personal circumstances, Ransome
chose his ex-wife's maiden name as surname for his fictional children. Hardyment observes that "the first hesitant notes for the story
are in a notebook, a 'Walker's Looseleaf Transfer Case,'" so it may
have been an authorial whim.)[1]

The Walkers are led (in both age and rank) by John, who is about
twelve years old in the first book. Sometimes seen as one of Ransome's *alter egos,* John is a serious, conscientious boy, perhaps a little
weighed down by responsibility. He sees himself as a stand-in for his
absentee father (who is in the Navy). Commander Walker passes on
his role to his son in the very famous telegram at the beginning of

Swallows and Amazons, which replies to the children's request that they should be allowed to camp, alone, on the island in the lake: "BETTER DROWNED THAN DUFFERS IF NOT DUFFERS WONT DROWN" (*SA,* 19). This pragmatism and sense of personal responsibility infuses the whole series of books.

John's sister, Susan, takes on the role of ship's "mate" to his "captain." She is cook, housekeeper, and surrogate mother, and she is occasionally satirized by her siblings for trying to treat a campsite like a kitchen.

The third Walker is Titty (a name that has occasionally caused a problem for readers and television producers in this less innocent age), who represents another side of Ransome's character. She is the dreamer, the sensitive and thoughtful child, who provides a certain mystic ballast to the earnest heartiness and wholesomeness of her family. Titty provides, in *Swallows and Amazons,* the imaginative links with Ransome's literary heritage; while her brothers and sisters treat the world as the playground that it is, she dreams of treasure islands, and she converts the "real" island into Robinson Crusoe's island. She thinks to herself, "That was the thing that spoilt *Robinson Crusoe.* In the end he came home. There ought never to be an end" (*SA,* 200).

Roger, who begins the saga by pretending to sail up the field to the lakeside farmhouse, is sketched as a stereotypical small boy, and through the series he develops least of all the characters (with the possible exception, as we shall see, of Peggy Blackett). His hero-worship of his elder brother is tempered slightly by a rebellious urge; Roger has a liking for engines in boats, whereas for the rest of the family, "Sail is the thing."

The youngest Walker, Bridget (known as "Vicky" in *Swallows and Amazons* because she was "like Queen Victoria in old age" [*SA,* 20]), does not emerge as an active character (a rather trenchant toddler) until the eighth book, *Secret Water.*

The Walkers' first sparring partners and friends are the Amazon Pirates, Nancy and Peggy Blackett, who live with their widowed mother at a lakeside house, "Beckfoot"; sail their own dinghy, *Amazon*; and have their own, rather different but no less secure middle-class, family mores. Both Nancy and Peggy suffer rather more than the Walkers from their initial portraits (possibly also because the Amazons are never the main "focalizers" of any of the books). Nancy is the "tomboy" (although it is never suggested that she is emulating boys per se); Peggy, her younger sister, is an eternal second-in-command, and despite a moment or two of glory in *Winter Holiday,* she remains a cipher. At the outset, however, it is Peggy who describes their situation. "'Her real name isn't Nancy,' said Peggy, 'Her name is Ruth, but Uncle Jim said that Amazons were ruthless, and as our ship is the *Amazon,* and we are Amazon pirates from the Amazon River, we had to change her name. Uncle Jim gave us the ship last year. We only had a rowing boat before that'" (*SA,* 117).

In the fourth book, *Winter Holiday,* the Swallows and the Amazons are at first seen from the point of view of two more children, son and daughter of a university academic (Ransome's father, it will be remembered, was a history professor). Dick Callum is the archetypical studious boy, a myopic, absent-minded, and faintly obsessive scientist. His sister, Dorothea, is one of Ransome's masterstrokes. She is a budding writer, but a writer deeply influenced by the wilder kinds of romantic fiction. Beside Titty, the mystic, she at first seems to be rather shallow, but she lives a happily conscious double life, paraphrasing the reality around her into the worst clichés of "ordinary" children's books, frequently to the amusement or mystification of her pragmatic peers. Together, "the D.'s" provide a refreshing and not always flattering gloss on the Swallows and the Amazons and provide another way into their exclusive world.

The only adult who could be added to the list of major regular players is Nancy and Peggy's Uncle Jim, known throughout as "Captain Flint." He is a fat, balding sailor and world traveler lately turned writer, who has returned to the Lake District of his youth. The element of self-portrait here is surprisingly astringent. Captain Flint begins as a faintly stagey uncle, but he is far from being bland. He is erratic in "real life," and, as the token adult in the three fantasy/romances (*Peter Duck, Missee Lee,* and *Great Northern?*) he is a flawed, unreliable, and thoroughly ambivalent character.

And what of the books themselves? Can a million words be usefully summarized in a paragraph or two? Clearly, the attraction of the Swallows' and Amazons' and D.'s' adventures is as much in the details as in the broad outlines of the plots; but those broad outlines will provide us with a useful map.

Swallows and Amazons is the first meeting of the Walkers and the Blacketts, and establishes much of the setting for the later books. The year is 1929, and the Walker family (complete with baby and nurse, but lacking father, who is stationed abroad with the Royal Navy) are on holiday at a farmhouse called Holly Howe, somewhere in the Lake District. The four elder children borrow a sailing boat, *Swallow,* and camp out on a small island in the middle of the lake, styling themselves explorers.

They encounter the "Amazon pirates," and together the children explore, make maps, and meet local characters, such as the charcoal burners. They have a "war," there is a storm, and much time is spent on the ordinary activities of camping, fishing, and sailing. There is also a subplot. Captain Flint's memoirs are stolen, and Titty finds them buried on a small island. This is as close as Ransome ever comes to the banal. Generally, there is little of the simple adventurousness and wild coincidence of which children's books had often previously been made.

The second book in the fictive sequence (although the third to be published) is *Peter Duck*. This is the first of Ransome's fantasies, a story that (we learn in the *next* book, *Swallowdale*) was supposedly made up by the Walkers and the Blacketts during the winter of 1929, while they were staying on a wherry on the Norfolk Broads with Captain Flint. (Among Ransome's papers is a first draft called "Their Own Story," which attempts to build a story from the children's contributions.)[2] *Peter Duck* is very much a pastiche of *Treasure Island*, with some of its moral ambiguity. However, the fact that it features the children from *Swallows and Amazons* produces some oddities of narrative and intent. By a curious irony, the children who seemed so real in a "real" world, now appear to be incongruous in a startlingly realized "fictional" world.

In the company of the old sailor, Peter Duck (based on Captain Sehmel of *Racundra*), Captain Flint and the children sail the North Atlantic in their schooner *Wild Cat* (named after the island on the lake) in search of long-buried treasure. They are pursued by the villainous Black Jake, in his black yacht, the *Viper*. On the island, where there are sharks and crabs, they experience a tropical storm and an earthquake, and narrowly escape as the *Viper* is destroyed by a waterspout. The treasure they find is suitably modest.

Swallowdale, set in the summer of the following year, returns us to "reality" and the Lake District; it is the longest of the books and has the most leisurely construction. The Swallows at first camp on Wild Cat Island, but then Captain John, much to his shame, wrecks *Swallow*. While *Swallow* is being repaired, the Swallows camp in Swallowdale, a small valley on the fells (complete with stream and cave). The Amazons are confined to home by Great-aunt Maria, a dragonish figure of Victorian vintage, who distresses Mrs. Blackett and intimidates Captain Flint. The plot, such as it is, deals with the Amazons' attempts to join in the Swallows' explorations. There is a mountain-climbing expedition; Roger twists his ankle and spends the night with charcoal burners; Titty (rather hysterically) attempts to get rid of the great-aunt with a wax voodoo doll. Above all, the human landscape of the Lake District is fleshed out with more local figures. At the end of the book, *Swallow* is repaired, the great-aunt departs, and normality is restored.

This authentic background is built upon in the next book, set a few months later, *Winter Holiday*. Ransome notes in the *Autobiography* that he had a "sort of tenderness" for this book, because it was based on his experiences during the Great Frost of 1895, when Windermere was frozen over: "Those weeks of clear ice with that background of snow-covered, sunlit, blue-shadowed hills were, forty years after, to give me a book called *Winter Holiday*" (*A,* 46–47).

The introduction of Dick and Dorothea allows Ransome a new perspective. The holidays are extended when Nancy catches mumps, and the other children sled and skate, build an igloo, and explore the snow-covered fells. The younger children (led by Dick with scientific zeal and exactitude) rescue a cragfast sheep; the older children invent a signaling system (based on Ransome's own system designed to talk to a neighboring fisherman); and they all contrive sailing sleds when the lake freezes over. Captain Flint does not appear until quite late in the book, which is just as well since his houseboat has been appropriated to act as the "Fram," the Norwegian explorer Nansen's ship (described in *Farthest North;* Ransome had met Nansen in 1921). The climax of the book is a somewhat overly contrived expedition to the "North Pole," which goes wrong because of a snowstorm.

Dick and Dorothea are the linking figures, rather than the focal figures, in *Coot Club,* set on the Norfolk Broads in the spring of the following year. The Broads are a 300-mile system of rivers and flooded peat cuttings stretching across the low lying fen country of Norfolk and Suffolk in eastern England; they were and are popular with holidaymakers. Here Ransome creates a new society of children. There are Tom Dudgeon, the son of a local doctor in the (real) village of Horning; his neighbors, twin girls, Port and Starboard (who never really come alive as characters); and three local boys, Bill, Pete, and Joe, sons of local boat builders, who play at pirates with an old ship's boat called the *Death and Glory.*

Collectively, the children form a bird-protection society, the Coot Club. As the book begins, they are particularly interested in protecting a nesting coot, distinguished by an unusual white feather. Unfortunately, a noisy and crass boatload of visitors, known throughout as the "Hullabaloos," moor their large motor cruiser (the fact that it is a motor cruiser is significant in Ransome's moral order of things) over the nest, and refuse to move. As the coot's eggs are in danger of not hatching, Tom breaks all the codes of sailing and local hospitality,

"LOWER AWAY"

and casts the cruiser adrift. He is then pursued (with perhaps an excess of obsession) all around the Broads.

Dick and Dorothea, who are staying with their mother's old nurse, Mrs. Barrable, and her pug dog, William, become involved. They learn to sail a little and have a comprehensive tour of the area (this time Ransome sticks to geographical fact), and, as with the Lake District novels, many local characters contribute. In a fine climax, the Hullabaloos, having wrecked their cruiser in a last manic attempt to catch Tom, are rescued from Breydon Water by the three small boys.

Ransome worried that displacing his characters to a different landscape would "do for" the books. But he was almost as at home in Norfolk as he was in the northwest, and he lovingly conjures up another world of children and adults and local people going about their daily lives. Like the Lake District, the Norfolk Broads have been damaged by the later twentieth century, and Ransome's meticulous portrait is an invaluable reminder of what has been lost.

If the most memorable feature of *Winter Holiday* is its brilliant evocation of the winter scene, *Pigeon Post* is at least partly memorable for its portrayal of a high, dry summer. We return to the Lake District, in the same year as *Coot Club,* where the Swallows and Amazons and "D.'s" are together, but temporarily without boats. Captain Flint is away prospecting for minerals in South America, and, for various plausible reasons, only Mrs. Blackett is in evidence. Consequently, the holiday begins with the children camping in Beckfoot orchard.

Nancy decides to spend their time prospecting for gold on the fells. (The hills of the Lake District have from earliest times been a source of a variety of minerals, notably copper, but also gold.) However, the children are not allowed to go any distance from the house, which they must do in order to prospect, because of the difficulty of communication in a world where telephones are rare. An acute water shortage and a constant danger of fire seem to prohibit camping. These problems are overcome in a very practical fashion.

The new hobby of the summer is keeping homing pigeons (called, with characteristic Ransome humor, Homer, Sophocles, and Sappho), and Dick invents a device (carefully illustrated) that allows homecoming pigeons to ring a bell, thus alerting the household. Titty's faintly romantic and mystic character is rather less plausibly exploited in her finding water at the perfect campsite on the edge of mining country, High Topps, by water divining (dowsing). Despite the tart (and utterly reasonable) opposition of the local farmer's wife, Mrs. Tyson, the children move from Beckfoot and set up camp beside their new well.

From then on, the pace is very rapid, as they try to find and smelt some gold before Captain Flint's return. They meet an old miner, Slater Bob; they suppose themselves in competition with a rival prospector ("Squashy Hat"). They find what they think is gold, build an elaborate furnace, and make charcoal. Dick becomes the lynchpin, the unlikely figure to whom the usual leaders, Nancy and John, turn for advice. In the best-paced climax of the series, Dick discovers that what they have found is not gold, but copper; careless tourists cause a spectacular fell fire, and one of the pigeons helps to alert the local fire-fighters. The rival prospector turns out to be Timothy, Captain Flint's shy partner. For sheer narrative skill and wealth of incident, *Pigeon Post* stands out in the series, and was a worthy recipient of the first Carnegie Medal.

The Ransomes lived for a time near the village of Pin Mill on the River Orwell on the east coast of England, the setting for the beginnings of both *We Didn't Mean to Go to Sea* and its sequel, *Secret Water*. (Not for the first time, reality and fiction overlapped. The Walkers stay with a Miss Powell, who, at one point, cooks omelettes for them. Subsequently, the real Miss Powell of Pin Mill, who also took in guests, was obliged to learn how to cook omelettes!)[3]

In *We Didn't Mean to Go to Sea* Ransome not only wrote his most exciting and convincing narrative, but he put the Walker children into "real" danger, which deepens and develops their characters. Immaculately paced and summing up much of what he has to say about sailing, codes of behavior, and childhood, the book has a strong claim to being Ransome's masterpiece.

The book builds up the children's necessary skills very slowly, in the manner of the folk-tale. As they are pottering about on the river (their father is due home from posting abroad, any day now) they meet a young sailor, Jim Brading, and are invited for a short (inland) trip on his "little white cutter with red sails," the *Goblin*. They moor in Harwich harbor and Jim rows ashore to get fuel for the engine. He doesn't return. Because of the children's inexperience, the *Goblin*'s anchor drags (all of this is narrated in a very low key) and they drift out into the North Sea, first in fog and later with an offshore wind. John realizes that to try to get back into the difficult harbor of Harwich in the dark and against the wind would be virtually impossible and probably disastrous. Despite Susan's seasick opposition, he sets sail and navigates out to sea, narrowly avoiding buoys and a steamship (the *Goblin* has no oil for her riding lights) and falling asleep at the tiller.

By daylight, the wind has dropped; they have survived. They pick up a kitten that is clinging to flotsam, and, approaching Holland, take on board a pilot, who is so impressed by their feat that he guides them into the harbor at Flushing for no fee. As they sail in, they pass the steamer that is carrying their father home. He sees them, manages to jump ship, and solves all their problems (in folk-tale fashion). They sail home together, to find that Jim Brading was knocked over by a bus and has been unconscious in hospital while they have been sailing, and that their mother does not know of their adventure. Whether the coincidence of the meeting with their father makes or destroys the book can be debated.

We Didn't Mean to Go to Sea is a tour de force; beside it, *Secret Water* is a gentle story of map-making in an enclosed and safe piece of water. In comparison with the wide, simple sweep of the plot and lack of control (on the part of the characters) of the previous book, *Secret Water* seems neat and calm.

The efficient Commander Walker, now appearing in the flesh, replaces the erratic Captain Flint as the resident manipulator of events. The Walker family cruising holiday is cancelled because of the navy, providing the book with one of the great opening lines: "The First Lord of the Admiralty was unpopular at Pin Mill."[4] Commander Walker sets up an expedition to map the tidal inlets near Walton-on-the-Naze, a series of small, muddy and reedy islands around Hamford Water (which is, Hardyment reports, now known locally as "Secret Water")[5].

The Swallows are provided with a boat, and improbably enough, Nancy and Peggy are imported to join them. This is the last time that the Swallows and Amazons appear together in a "realistic" book, probably because Nancy's games sit rather tiresomely beside the attitudes of the newly mature Walkers. Ransome also creates, perhaps with his least success, another established society of children and boats, the "Eels," a group not entirely pleased to find explorers on their territory.

As several critics have noted, the masterstroke of the book is that Bridget, now aged about four, accompanies them, solidifying the family structure. Bridget participates in a game of savages and human sacrifice, and with Titty and Roger is caught (perhaps inevitably) by the tide.

Despite such distractions, the map that the children make, beautifully drawn and meticulously added to throughout the book, is completed by the deadline. Yet it is clear that, for the Swallows at least, the limits of play are rapidly being reached.

"1931" is a busy fictional year. That autumn, we find ourselves back at the village of Horning on the Norfolk Broads. The cast for

The Big Six has now been rather sensibly reduced to Tom and the three Death and Glories, and Dick and Dorothea. *The Big Six* is named after a legendary team of detectives, said to have operated in the twenties and thirties (at least in detective fiction) from London's police headquarters, Scotland Yard. There is a title-page epigraph: "'But who are the Big Six?' asked Pete. 'It's the Big Five really,' said Dorothea. 'They are the greatest detectives in the world. They sit in their cubby-holes in Scotland Yard and solve one mystery after another.' 'But why Six?' 'There are only five of them and there are six of us,' said Dorothea."

The book begins at the end of the boating season, when the *Death and Glory,* now fitted out with a cabin from the proceeds of the salvage at the end of *Coot Club,* lies peacefully at Horning Staithe. But then boats begin to be cast adrift at night, and suspicion falls on the boys; they try to avoid the problem by mooring elsewhere, but wherever they go, more boats are cast adrift. Dick and Dorothea arrive and start to collect clues—evidence from local boys, cycle tracks in the mud, a scrap of trouser material. This may sound like a conventional "children's adventure," especially as the culprit is obvious to the reader from a very early stage. However, as with all of Ransome's books, there are no short-cuts. Just as all sailing must be achieved in the face of winds that blow and water that potentially drowns, so detecting must go on in the face of the disgust of the adult boat-building community and the necessity of producing genuine legal evidence. That evidence is finally completed with the aid both of a friendly angler (all brothers of the angle form a freemasonry, regardless of age) and of Dick's new hobby, photography (with 1930s technology).

The Big Six is a considerable novel in the detective genre. Not only does it draw together all Ransome's skills of construction and, in effect, narrative theory, but the scenes of fishing and sailing are neatly integrated into the plot. A testimony to Ransome's democratic view of English society, it also provides a nice contrast between the romantic and literary Dorothea and the pragmatic boys for whom the situation is unpleasant reality.

Reality is a long way away in *Missee Lee,* an exuberant farrago in which Ransome returns to the manner (and, it is usually assumed, the same fictional method of composition) as *Peter Duck.* The difference is that this is no pastiche; *Missee Lee* is a totally original work, set in the China that Ransome knew in the 1920s. The nominal Swallows and Amazons, sailing around the world with the erratic Captain Flint, lose their ship (pet monkey, gasoline, fire) and are captured by Chinese pirates. The pirates' leader, Missee Lee, is trying against much opposition to take over her father's role. She is a true literary original (although she may have been based on Mrs. Sun Yat-sen).

Missee Lee has had to interrupt her Cambridge education in classics (she coxed the second eight at Newnham College). But given a truly captive audience, she begins to teach Latin to the reluctant children (and the even more reluctant Captain Flint), to fulfill her frustrated academic ambitions. There is a nice irony in Roger's being the most successful pupil and Nancy and Captain Flint the least. Some time is spent on the political machinations of the three pirate leaders (shades of Ransome's political past) and although the plot may creak, it creaks in what seems to be an authentic atmosphere, and builds up to an exciting escape. Missee Lee is tempted to leave with them, but finally returns to her pirate duty, her ambition motivated at least in part by a feminist scorn for her male rivals.

The book has the same moral and ethical difficulties as *Peter Duck,* but is more than acceptable as a page-turner and is notable for its authentic backgrounds and its constant quirks of characterization.

The final Lake District book—and, in a sense, the true end of the series, is *The Picts and the Martyrs; or, Not Welcome at All.* (The subtitle seems to refer to the plot, but may equally refer to the whole book. Ransome was increasingly depressive about his novels, and Evgenia increasingly damning of them. *The Picts and the Martyrs* was published only through the encouragement of his mother.)[6]

This is "1932." The D.'s arrive at Beckfoot to stay with Nancy and Peggy while their mother is away. She is convalescing from influenza: "Her brother . . . had taken her off for a sea voyage and a cruise around the coasts of Scandinavia" (*PM,* 9)—a very Ransome-ish choice of holiday. Great-aunt Maria (of *Swallowdale*), hears of Molly Blackett's absence, and feels that it is her duty to look after her greatnieces. Nancy, afraid that the presence of guests will aggravate the "G.A."'s uncertain temper even further, persuades the D.'s to decamp to an old hut in the woods, to become "Picts" while Nancy and Peggy return to duty and smart frocks and become "Martyrs."

Like *Swallowdale,* some of the tension is derived from keeping the D.'s a secret, but much of the interest is in their education. They learn quite a few things about survival and a lot about the local inhabitants. They are taught to catch trout by a farmer's boy (Jacky, also from *Swallowdale*), learn to handle their own new boat (the *Scarab*), and help Captain Flint's partner, Timothy (from *Pigeon Post*), with his assays from their mine. (He is living aboard the houseboat, and the Great Aunt, who has caught sight of him once, suspects him of being a dangerous tramp.) The combination of these circumstances involves Dick in burgling Beckfoot to get hold of necessary analytical chemicals.

The two great virtues of the book are the emergence of Dick and Dorothea as central, initiated characters and the cumulation of the drawing of background scenes and people. The cook becomes a central character, and we meet the doctor, the postman, the policeman, a passing butcher, Mary Swainson (from *Swallowdale*), and so on. They are not all approving, but they all treat the children as peers (another of Ransome's great appeals).

The climax of the book is an excellent example of Ransome's use of parallel narratives (after virtuoso performances in *Pigeon Post* and *The Big Six*). Aunt Maria disappears. She suspects that the Swallows may be around and goes in search of them, ending up at the houseboat. Timothy, fortunately, is not there. The whole countryside is raised, and she is eventually discovered by Dick and Dorothea, who are obliged, incognito, to bring her home. They slip away as she is greeted by her pursuers, and Nancy's scheme is successful.

The Picts and the Martyrs ends just as the Swallows are about to arrive for another boating holiday, and by now, all the characters have grown up to the point at which a deeper formation of relationships would be inevitable. But instead, Ransome, with, as we shall see, the assistance of his friends, turned to a final fantasy to complete the series: *Great Northern?*

This is in many ways a disappointing finale. A tale of ornithology and an unpleasant ornithologist in the Scottish Hebrides, it deals with what is now a very fashionable subject, conservation. But it has all the disadvantages of the "fantasy" mode Ransome used in *Peter Duck* and *Missee Lee* plus the obvious problem that the oldest children are now well into their teens, and yet behave as if they were still pre-pubescent. The meticulous Hebredean setting should not mislead us into assuming that the plot line bears any relationship to reality.

The Swallows, Amazons, and D.'s are cruising with Captain Flint on a borrowed boat, the *Sea Bear*. While the senior children are helping Captain Flint to scrub the boat's bottom, Dick comes across a nesting pair of Great Northern Divers, rare birds known to nest only seldom, if at all, in the Hebrides. The desire of Captain Flint for a quiet life is ruined by an unscrupulous egg collector, who wishes to shoot the birds as evidence. Dick equally wishes only to take a picture and to leave the birds in peace.

In order to give Dick a chance, the others set off as decoys, only to incur the wrath of the local Scots, who think that they are deliberately disturbing the deer. Justice and honor win, and the birds are photographed and survive. But the characters are now little more than gestures, and their behavior is stereotyped and much younger than the developing characters of *We Didn't Mean to Go to Sea,* or *The Picts and the Martyrs.* Ransome's immense skill at handling both the climax and the parallel narratives is wasted on a plot that requires the characters to be singularly obtuse.

The story of the Swallows and Amazons and their friends might seem to end there. But among the manuscripts in the Arthur Ransome collection at Abbott Hall, Kendal, Ransome's biographer found part of another story, which he called "Coots in the North" and published in 1988.

This fragment consists of the first four chapters and parts of a synopsis and centers on the Death and Glories. It opens at the Staithe in Horning, much troubled by the crowds of visitors, who constantly get themselves into trouble.

> Joe, Bill, and Pete of the Salvage company spent a good deal
> of time, when aboard and not at school, in getting boats
> afloat that had gone aground . . . but visitors were much too
> ready to think that everyone else was doing things for fun
> as they were themselves, and the Salvage Company often
> toiled earnestly and well, only to see the rescued visitors sail
> away with no more than a cheerful "Thank you", while the
> salvage men coiled their ropes, wiped the sweat from their
> faces, and spat gloomily into the water. (*CN,* 105)

They stow away on a cruiser that is being transported by lorry to the Lake District, and are left behind. The main fragment ends as they meet up with Dick and Dorothea and Nancy, and the synopsis suggests various incidents before they save Captain Flint's houseboat from running aground in a storm and earn their passage south. Certainly Ransome's choice of his three young protagonists seems a promising one, and the prose is as sharp as ever, but whether he would have been able to reconcile the growth and development of the Swallows and Amazons that we have seen with holiday activities, let alone the working-class pragmatism of the boys, is difficult to say.

This, then, has been an outline of the sequence on which Ransome's reputation rests; the following four chapters explore the books in more detail.

5

The Lake District Novels

When Arthur Ransome began to write the "Swallows and Amazons" books, he had served a long apprenticeship. Not only had his style been refined to a Defoe-like functionalism, but he had retained a childlike way of looking at life, reflected in his precise interest in the practical. That is, his writing always has a single focus; he is never (like, for example, A. A. Milne or T. H. White) writing with one eye on an adult reader. His claim, repeated several times, that he wrote for himself, may seem disingenuous, and Aidan Chambers has pointed out that "no one, surely, can believe that, had Ransome been writing for adults—in the sense of an implied adult reader—he would have adopted the tone of voice so evident and so well-created in *Swallows and Amazons*."[1] Yet all the biographical evidence suggests that Ransome approached his occupations (one can hardly call them hobbies) with a single-mindedness and innocence characteristic of the best of childhood, or of nature mysticism.

His interest in skills is very reminiscent of Kipling, who was another craftsman with a deep respect for the countryside and its people. An anonymous critic in the London *Times Literary Supplement* wrote in 1950 of Ransome's "curious ability not merely to sympathise with a child's point of view but to see things from that point of view for himself. More fundamentally, however, he succeeds in being serious because he is writing about a serious subject."[2]

This seriousness extended to his love and intimate knowledge of the places he wrote about and his democratic identification with and acceptance of the local people. This democratic feeling means that the narrator and the fictional adults in his books accord the fictional children (and, therefore, the child readers) equal respect.

Similarly, his love of family, childhood, and parental figures was combined with a moral code which rested in mutual care and responsibility. For example, the epigraph to chapter 4 of *Swallowdale* is from Pope's translation of Homer's *Odyssey*. "By mutual confidence and mutual aid/Great deeds are done and great discoveries made."[3] Richard Jefferies, who had links with the same literary tradition, used the same translation of the *Odyssey* as the underlying text in *Bevis*. For Ransome, the quotation has associations with both national and family codes of behavior.

Even the most incidental of the fictional children are part of families with subtle relationships, and private languages and modes of behavior. Significantly, one of the few thoroughly unpleasant characters in his books—George Owdon of *Coot Club* and *The Big Six*—has, it seems, only an uncle, not parents.[4] Similarly, Ransome's subconsciously ambivalent attitude to his father is continually sublimated, either by attitudes or incidents; for most of the books the fathers are far away (in the case of the Walkers), or preoccupied (Professor Callum), or simply a memory (Bob Blackett is, we assume, dead).

This insistence on the integrity of the family may account for some of his books' longevity. A modern critic, Michelle Landsberg, has noted that although as a "lower middle-class urban Canadian child" she had little in common with the children in the books, she nevertheless found John Walker to be a great influence: "His sense of deep obligation to a moral code, part naval and part familial, was expressed so compellingly in his speech and actions that until my midteens he was a sort of internalized exemplar for me."[5]

By modern children's book standards, Ransome's children are extremely taciturn about their real feelings. As Geoffrey Trease has observed, "There is a breezy healthiness about his stories which is at times suspiciously suggestive of antiseptic. These children are so busy hauling in and belaying that they seem untroubled by dreams or problems of personal relationship. They take plenty of soundings at sea, but they plumb no emotional depths."[6] This judgment underestimates them. Not only do they reflect a culture that is traditionally reticent, but they are, to some extent, what they do; they express themselves through action rather than analysis. Their emotions can therefore be understood without the embarrassment or awkwardness of spoken words. In this, one might suspect, Ransome was a shrewd child psychologist.

Similarly, codes are necessary to the growing child—"Rigid social rules help . . . because they offer convenient, arbitrary measures of approved behaviour"[7]—and Ransome, drawing on his own childhood, reflects the codes of an older social order. As Fred Inglis has pointed out, "Ransome takes life seriously, unselfconsciously so; and . . . therefore the actions of his characters are important, not just for themselves, but because they are principled."[8]

In short, looking at Ransome's achievement in the "Swallows and Amazons" series, it is easy to see how the Ransome virtues—family, honor, skill, good sense, responsibility and mutual respect—interact. In reading *Swallows and Amazons* and its successors, then, it is very illuminating to pursue these interlinked themes and principles, but there is a second organizational factor that groups the novels: the idea of place.

This chapter will look at the five books set in the English Lake District: *Swallows and Amazons* (fictional year 1), *Swallowdale* and *Winter Holiday* (fictional year 2), *Pigeon Post* (fictional year 3), and *The Picts and the Martyrs* (fictional year 4). Together they demonstrate the development of the self-referential life of the series, moving from "new" characters to an established society. "Behind" the action of the books, and forming an integral part of their fabric, is Ransome's portrait of the landscape and people of the Lake District. Ransome creates a complete world, from a child's-eye view.

Using *Swallows and Amazons* as the exemplar, I therefore look first at the structures of the novels and the way they reflect parental control, then at the family codes expressed and the way they emerge through the interaction of characters. Beside these major topics can be placed Ransome's insistence upon skill and craft, his re-creation of the Lake District as an integral part of the books, and, finally, the web of literary associations on which he draws.

Swallows and Amazons

Structure and Family

Ransome seems to have approached writing as he did sailing or fishing; certain things would work for logical reasons, provided they were done well. Consequently, the structural patterns that can be clearly seen in his novels may not have been deliberate, but they certainly reflect an unconsciously highly skilled narrator, and they are entirely appropriate to the narrative content.

His interest in the theory of narrative structure, which perhaps shows him to be a critic ahead of his time, is demonstrated in the

structuralist summary of *Swallows and Amazons* (1930) in a letter
to his friend Margaret Renold in 1934:

> The essential point of a plot is a change of relationship be-
> tween the characters. Some kind of stresses and strains
> have to be set up between hero or heroes and other children
> or grown ups. That is my real problem. E.g. in S and A;
> S. v. A. S v Cap. F. S. and A v. Cap. F. All the lot v. burglars.
> Billies v burglars and pro Cap. F. S and A and Cap F all in
> the same boat [i.e., in the same situation]. You see what I
> mean. The story such as it is puts into the concrete one after
> another of a series of different relationships.[9]

Similarly, as the novels progress—and the Lake District novels
form an interesting unit in this respect—they form for their readers,
even more than for their characters, a bildungsroman.[10] As we shall
see, the *closure* that is so characteristic of books for younger children
is strong in *Swallows and Amazons* and progressively weakens.
Swallows and Amazons is notably circular: it begins and ends with
the same character in the same place. Although *Swallowdale* ends
with Susan's remark, "Isn't it a blessing to get home?" (*S,* 453), they
are not at home, but on their own island. *Winter Holiday* and *Pigeon
Post* both end away from home, but in the comforting presence of
adults, after great danger. *The Picts and the Martyrs* is a book most
concerned with displacement and disruption, and it ends without the
restitution of normality. These structural patterns are integral with
the freedom that Ransome gives his children and the limits that he
imposes.

From the beginning, the Walkers' mother establishes the limits of
freedom. She stipulates not only where they shall be, but also orders
small details. "'No medicines. . . . Anyone who wants doctoring is in-
valided home.' 'If it's really serious,' said Titty, 'but we can have a
plague or a fever or two by ourselves'" (*SA,* 32–33). (This concern for
their safety does not, as Tucker points out, extend to being careful
with bows and arrows or wearing lifejackets, but Ransome was a
man of his time, a time when such things were not considered.)[11]

Suitably provided for, the children sail to the island; Mother comes
to check on them before they go to sleep and brings more food. The
next morning, after only a single uneventful night, John and Roger
sail back to Holly Howe to report (and find it an oddly alien place).

Whenever there is a problem, or a difficulty, psychological closure
is applied by a compensation. When John is accused by Captain Flint
of lying—which is, of course, to be accused of breaking a fundamental

code—he first applies a suitably ruralistic philosophy ("But the big hills far up the lake helped to make him feel that the houseboat man did not matter. The hills had been there before Captain Flint. They would be there for ever." [*SA*, 178]), and then physical therapy (he swims around the island). But the real healing comes when Mother appears once again for Vicky's birthday party.

Mother is therefore a great link with the rest of the world. She knows all about the children's troubles with the houseboat and reacts very calmly to John's distress, in a somewhat Victorian way: "'It doesn't matter what people think or say if they don't know you. They may think anything'" (*SA*, 85).

Similarly, whenever the children are in danger, or there is some real displacement, she is there. When Titty is left alone on the island and is playing at being Robinson Crusoe, Mother comes and cooks her a meal. After the night-sailing episode, when John, Susan, and Roger have been in genuine danger of drowning, she comments, "Don't you think that was very nearly like being duffers?" (*SA*, 265). Her forgiveness is not simply a proxy for the omnipotent father figure of Commander Walker (although she is lower in the sexist hierarchy); it is part of the family code:

> Captain John came home [i.e., to the island].
> His first words were, "I told mother about our being out all last night and not coming home till to-day."
> "Was she very upset about it?" said Susan.
> "I think she was rather, inside. But she hid it, and it's all right now. Only, I've promised not to do it again."
> After that, Susan cheered up and became much less like a native and more like a mate. (*SA*, 269)

After the big climactic storm, when a tent collapses and the children fantasize in the best literary manner about the loss of their ship, they receive a massive reinforcement of security: "And then came the natives." First the local farmer's wife, Mrs. Dixon, with her bucket of porridge ("'This really is eating out of the common dish,' said Titty" [*SA*, 361]), and then both mothers. The reaction of the children mixes an appreciation of reality with a demonstration of family loyalty:

> After they were gone the Swallows and Amazons looked at each other. . . .
> "It's the natives," said Nancy. "Too many of them. They turn everything into a picnic."
> "Mother doesn't," said Titty.

"Nor does ours when she's alone," said Nancy. . . . "It's
when they all get together. . . . They can't help themselves,
poor things." (*SA*, 367)

The strength of this relationship between adults and children and
its structural effect are both so clear that it is curious that many
critics have overlooked it. John Rowe Townsend, in what is in many
ways the British standard work on children's literature, *Written for
Children*, says, "We may wish we could see [the children] in a living
relationship with their parents, instead of having the parents mainly
as understanding figures in the background."[12] Juliet Dusinberre, in
her study of childrens' books and radical experiments in art, *Alice to
the Lighthouse*, notes in passing, "The child unhampered by parents
has become a commonplace of twentieth-century children's books
since Arthur Ransome."[13] Crouch in *The Nesbit Tradition* suggests
that "one might feel a theoretical regret that Ransome did not choose
to show children and adults in partnership."[14] (In an extreme mis-
reading, Crouch goes on to suggest that most of the adults are "hostile and barbarous.")

All of this is quite untrue, for throughout the book the adults are
very much there, providing security. Fred Inglis, possibly the most
authoritative of contemporary politically orientated British critics,
notes, however, that "Arthur Ransome . . . wrote of the absolute
safety of a Lake District (and Norfolk Broads) bounded by the absolute justice of the parental writ."[15]

Ransome's young children, then, are in the ideal circumstance;
they have an idyllic playground and a sense of place: in the hills, in
the family, and in the moral order of things. The hills that ring the
lake, with their heather-covered slopes above the woods, are a secure
boundary, rather like the hills that enclose the Thames valley in *The
Wind in the Willows*. (In *Coot Club*, Dorothea cites Mr. Toad.[16]) Consequently, the children can play and grow within known limits, and
there is a great deal more to the book than Joan Aiken's summary of
its moral message: "How to get along without parents just the same
as if they were there."[17]

Family Codes and Characters
Probably the most common accusation of those who feel that children's literature is a contradiction in terms is that child characters
are necessarily limited. Do the Swallows and Amazons themselves
escape from this stricture, or are they submerged by the twin re-
straints of public and family role?

John Walker is initially the rather priggish, solemn, bland boy,
very much under his father's shadow—a boy who, when rowing "navy

stroke," made it "a point of honour that the oars should not splash when they went into the water" (*SA*, 173). One of the recurrent motifs is his references to his father; he carries his books as totems, and he quotes him in moments of need. For example, when they are, unwisely, sailing at night, he says, "Even Daddy used to say, 'Never be ashamed to reef a small boat in the dark'" (*SA*, 255). As Margery Fisher observes: "John . . . is such a sturdy, dependable, extrovert boy that one would be tempted to think that Arthur Ransome meant him as a type . . . [But] he shows an increasing sense of responsibility and a practical good sense that saves him from appearing to the reader as a complete prig."[18]

In a sense, John's part is necessarily ambivalent to the adult, but understandable to the child. His relationship to adults is possibly the most realistic of all the characters. He does not expect them to be nice; they are in a different, authoritative world.

Susan, the domestic, occupies a place similar to her mother in the family hierarchy. (It is worth noting—although it may jar for the modern reader—that mother "without leave from daddy, could [not] let them go alone" [*SA*, 18].) She provides a firm undercurrent of responsibility that unfortunately makes her character rather intractable. In *Swallowdale* and *Pigeon Post,* her motherly role becomes a cliché for both the reader and the other characters. She is not, however, above a mild criticism of the Captain: "'Lucky we brought a sailmaker's needle.' 'Luckier if you knew how to use it,' said the mate a moment or two later, when she looked up and saw the captain sucking his thumb" (*SA*, 278). Susan's domestic efforts are never actually ridiculed by author or characters; they are taken quite seriously by the other children.

So is Titty. She is the romantic, who reads *Robinson Crusoe* when she is alone on the island, and stands looking out over the storm-swept lake and getting soaked to the skin. But like her siblings, she comes to life most subtly in her interactions with other members of the family.

Roger, similarly, is most convincing at moments such as that on Octopus lagoon, in the dark, when the oars are tangled in water-lilies: "'Perhaps they are octopuses,' said Roger. 'Titty read to me about how they put their arms out long, and grab people even out of a boat.' In Roger's voice there were clear signs of panic in the forecastle. Captain John took command at once" (*SA*, 231–32).

On the whole, the children's fears and loyalties are straightforward, because they understand the underlying value of skills and honor. Like E. Nesbit before him and William Mayne in our own day, Ransome implies the complexity of relationships by small touches. This is especially the case when the Walker family is contrasted with the Blacketts. Increasingly, as the series progresses, their codes conflict.

The Amazons, in this book, are perhaps the most crudely stereo-typed characters; they develop only as the landscape and people-scapes to which they belong also develop. (By *The Picts and the Martyrs,* Nancy and Peggy can be understood in a complex context.) In *Swallows and Amazons,* it is family, and family differences, that provides their identity.

For example, John and Nancy have different views of the future: Nancy, the child's child, proposes to live on the island all the year round; John, the adult's child, quietly puts down such nonsense: "I shall be going to sea some day . . . and so will Roger. But we'll always come back here on leave" (*SA,* 368). Similarly, John takes a quiet pleasure in the fact that the Amazons (despite their local knowledge) cannot translate the naval "four bells of the middle watch" (*SA,* 349).

Susan takes some time to realize that the interaction with adults is rather different in the Blackett–Turner household from that in the Walkers'. Mrs. Blackett, "a very little woman, not really much bigger than Nancy" (*SA,* 363) is not the calm mother that Mrs. Walker is; nor, as we see in the rare glimpse of adult life in *Swallowdale,* is her domestic life as smooth. Thus, when Captain Flint chases Nancy back to the island to apologize, Susan does not immediately under-stand what is going on.

> "I say, Susan," [John] shouted, "Captain Flint is coming after her."
> "You're as bad as Titty with her treasure," said Susan. "Natives don't do things like that."
> "But he is," said John. (*SA,* 291)

More seriously, Nancy and Peggy's standard of honesty is perhaps not quite as rigid as that of the Swallows, which possibly makes them more alive for today's reader. Nancy at one point says, "And there's lots to eat. We brought a plum pudding to cut up in pieces, and fry. Most luscious. Cook gave it to us. And then afterwards we found a cold tongue. It had hardly been touched, so we brought it too. But we came away rather privately because we thought we might be stopped" (*SA,* 298).

Such differences are precursors of the major difficulties that mark the end of their relationship in *Secret Water.* It may also be that, as the Walkers are, initially, the focalized family, we tend to see things from their point of view. In *Winter Holiday* and *The Picts and the*

Martyrs, the D.'s tend to dominate. Only in *Pigeon Post* is there equality of viewpoint, and even then the book begins with the Walkers. The Amazons, despite their strong presence, are never central to any of the books from the point of view of narrative, and this lack reflects on their characters.

Nancy's simple character suffers slightly from her involvement in the uncharacteristically melodramatic plot of *Swallows and Amazons.* She is rude, or at least spoiled and superior, to Sammy the policeman. Ransome makes the excuse that she has known him all her life (*SA,* 280), but his dismissal and subsequent apology smack very much of a lesser kind of children's book. This relationship has none of the mutual respect shown elsewhere.

Ransome has a good eye for the minutiae of behavior—perhaps especially of small children. For example, when Vicky has her second birthday, on the island, she brings her lamb and her elephant with her. "Vicky had her elephant with her. She forgot her lamb in the boat, and it had to be fetched later. Vicky liked the elephant better than the lamb because it was smaller. The lamb was so large that it was always being put down and forgotten" (*SA,* 182).

Outdoor Skills

The family codes and standards of behavior are also expressed practically and pragmatically: the skills of sailing and camping and fishing are skills of craft and love. To understand and to achieve them is to be initiated into a very select club. Some of the appeal of *Swallows and Amazons* may well lie precisely in the vicarious pleasure that the audience can take in being admitted into these circles. In a very important sense, the family unit is like the skilled group.

Of course, the sailing elements will exclude as many children as they will attract. Although Ransome's prose is consistently simple and uncluttered, his approach to describing boats can easily leave readers out of their depths. Or it may be that the language has its own special savor. In early examples, we can note how Ransome slips into the confidential second person: "John and Susan had done plenty of sailing, but there is always something to learn about a boat that you have not sailed before. . . . A lot of people do not know how to skull over the stern of a boat, but it is easy enough if you do know, and John had been taught by his father long ago in Falmouth harbour. The only trouble is that the nose of the boat waggles a bit from side to side" (*SA,* 53–54). This complicity may not appeal to everyone. When the small sailing dinghy, *Swallow,* is first described, one might be forgiven for abandoning all hope, especially when Ransome does supply *some* explanation, clearly implying that the rest of what he is talking about is obvious:

> "She doesn't seem to have a forestay," said John. "And there isn't a place to lead the halyard to in the bows to make it do instead."
> "Let me have a look," said Queen Elizabeth [their mother is temporarily in this role]. . . . "Is there a cleat under the thwart where the mast is stepped?"
> "Two," said John, feeling. The mast fitted in a hole in the forward thwart, the seat near the bows of the boat. It had a square foot, which rested in a slot cut to fit it in the kelson. (*SA*, 29)

But when they are setting the sail for the first time, Ransome is, somewhat awkwardly, forced to insert a gloss into a line of dialogue: "Is that what those blocks (pulleys) are for hooked to a ring in the kelson . . . ?" (*SA*, 29)

Perhaps the detail that most adults remember most vividly from childhood reading is the ability of Susan and Peggy to light fires with only sticks and moss and leaves. (For a meticulous description, see *SA*, 160–61). This particular achievement is elevated in *Winter Holiday* to a positively excluding skill: to use paper to light fires is a social solecism.

People and Places

Swallows and Amazons was, as Margery Fisher writes, "by no means the first English holiday-adventure, but it brought to a tired, bland genre a new exuberance in narrative and circumstance, an emphasis on practical techniques . . . and a positive affirmation of the way children could absorb and adapt to new places and events."[19]

Integral with the sense of detail is the sense of the people. Bob Dixon, in his book on sexism and racism, *Catching them Young,* places Ransome in the "exclusively middle-class" tradition of Nesbit: "if members of the lower classes appear at all, it's decidedly on the fringe."[20] There is some truth in this, but, as we have seen, Ransome was studiously democratic. *Everyone,* in one sense, is peripheral to the children's viewpoint.

Nonetheless, this is a "middle-class" book, and the characters use the middle-class dialect of the period: "I say" and "Look here" are endemic. But it is not always easy to distinguish among period, class, and family dialect—as when Peggy speaks of using the water breaker (or barrel) "as a puncheon for feastable drinks" (*SA*, 124). Also, the Amazons have a cook, the Swallows have a nurse; the farmers and farmers' wives form a kind of retinue. But they are far from being caricatures (as the working classes are in the second Carnegie Medal winner in 1937, Eve Garnett's *The Family from One End Street*);[21] they are people in their own right, and the children have to respect this individuality.

The nurse, for example, when John and Roger report back on the first morning, "somehow did not seem to feel that she was talking with seamen from other lands" (*SA*, 74). Mr. Jackson, the "powerful native" from Holly Howe, stands silently (and very expressive the silence is, too, in class terms), while Mrs. Walker talks gobbledegook with her children (*SA*, 64–65). Mr. Dixon, who provides continuity with *Swallowdale* and has quite a large part to play in *Winter Holiday*, is even more taciturn: "Mr. Dixon, who was waiting down by the boat, had said 'Good morning,' when he came, and now he said 'Good day to you,' as he rowed Mrs. Dixon away. He was always a very silent native" (*SA*, 364).

The children are treated well, but not indulged, either by parents or "natives." After the storm, "Nancy wanted to take the hay out of the haybags to make a last blaze on the camp fire. 'Nay,' said Mr. Jackson, 'it's good hay that.' So it was spared to be eaten by cows" (*SA*, 366).

The charcoal-burners—Ransome's own clay-pipe-bakers—are the same. The Swallows visit them on a day of calm, leaving blazes and patterans in the wood in the best literary exploring fashion. Ransome describes the process of charcoal-burning (to be used, initially, for keeping the campfire alight overnight, and, more spectacularly, for helping in the smelting in *Pigeon Post*) and the two ancient men (Old Billy and Young Billy), with their adder (or viper) that they keep for luck. On Ransome's principle that everything should be relevant, this incident becomes structural. The Billies have a message for Captain Flint, and their approach to the children is quite unsentimental:

> "Shall you be seeing those lasses again? . . . Well, you can tell them to tell their Uncle Jim . . ."
> "They can't," Titty broke in, "they're at war with him."
> "They'll tell him right enough." (*SA*, 155)

The people are set in, and form part of, the landscape. As Inglis points out, "Ransome mattered fundamentally because I saw him also as a celebrant of the great world of home. The splendour and detail of his stories, taking place . . . in an unending and paradisal holiday, were woven from a love of the landscape."[22]

Ransome never makes the common error of cutting the landscape down to child-size. The view may be myopic (it is not so much adults who are cut out of Ransome's books, but other children), but it is real. The evocations of the area never intrude; they are sketched only, forming a subtle background to the details of food and stores and activity. But they can also act as Ransome's most effective atmospheric passages when they are functional. For example, there is the children's first glimpse of the charcoal-burners, from the lake, at night.

> Suddenly high in the darkness they saw a flicker of bright flame. There was another and then another, and then a pale blaze lighting a cloud of smoke. They all looked up towards it as if they were looking at a little window, high up in a black wall. As they watched, the figure of a man jumped into the middle of the smoke, a black, active figure, beating at the flames. The flames died down, and it was as if a dark blind were drawn over the little window. . . .
> "It's savages," said Titty. "I was sure there must be some somewhere in the woods." (SA, 138)

Of course, Titty's reference to "savages," along with the children's consistent reference to adults as "natives," is part of an affectionate parody of desert island books from *Robinson Crusoe* onwards, and of the empire-building adventures in books by Henty, Ballantyne, and their ilk.

The Literary Tradition
Thus, it is important to see *Swallows and Amazons* as being part of, and deriving some of its density from, a literary tradition. The book begins with a literary reference, the epigraph to the first chapter:

> Or like stout Cortez, when with eagle eyes,
> He stared at the Pacific—and all his men
> Looked at each other with a wild surmise—
> Silent, upon a peak in Darien.

These lines from Keats's "On First Looking into Chapman's Homer" (the source is not given) are perhaps another unconscious link with that other major formative children's book, Richard Jefferies's *Bevis*.
   Part of that epic of boyhood involves Bevis and his friend Mark in building a hut and living on an island on a lake for over a week. They construct a gun that works (Jefferies gives meticulous instructions), and kill a disconcertingly large number of birds with it; they catch fish; they cook; they learn (at immense length) to sail. It is a book that, on the surface, celebrates the amorality of childhood as well as

freedom and self-reliance. Yet it is underpinned by a sense of responsibility and tradition.

To say that Ransome owes something to Jefferies is not to suggest imitation, although it is true that in both books there is a lake, an island, sailing, fishing, and a resolutely practical air. Rather it is that Ransome and Jefferies shared a romantic and practical love of nature and of country skills, and a very similar literary heritage.

A comparison of the books that Bevis, and the Swallows, take to their respective islands is fascinating. Bevis's collection is perhaps a little more intellectual than the Walkers': "The 'Odyssey,' Don Quixote, the grey and battered volume of ballads [Percy's *Reliques*], a tiny little book of Shakespeare's poems . . . and Filmore's rhymed translation of Faust. He found two manuscript books for the journal; these and the pens and ink-bottle could all go together in the final cargo."[23] The ship's library of the *Swallow* includes Titty's *Robinson Crusoe* ("It tells you just what to do on an island"); likewise, "John took *The Seaman's Handybook,* and Part Three of *The Baltic Pilot*. Both books had belonged to his father, but John took them with him even on holidays. Mate Susan took *Simple Cooking for Small Households*" (*SA*, 33).

Quite apart from confirming the typecasting, it is significant that Defoe should strike the keynote for *Swallows and Amazons,* as contrasted with the more fantastic Homer for *Bevis*. Yet, as we have seen, Ransome quotes Homer in *Swallowdale,* while his ballad-epigraphs to the second and third chapters of *Swallows and Amazons* are matched by Bevis's quotations from "King Estmere" and Longfellow's "Secret of the Sea."

Other, more important parallels exist between *Bevis* and *Swallows and Amazons* (and the first few chapters of *Swallowdale*). The children live in a dual world of fiction and reality; the fiction is of the late nineteenth-century kind, of wild adventure, often maritime and in an empire-building context.[24] Titty makes most conscious use of it, but the mood, or technique, is first announced by Roger.

In the first scene, he has been pretending to be a sailing ship in the meadow. His mother gives him the famous telegram, and "kissed him, anchored as he was" (*SA*, 17). Roger then sails away. "When he came out of the field into the wood he stopped being a sailing vessel. No one can sail through a pinewood. He became an explorer, left behind by the main body, following their trail through the forest, and keeping a sharp look out lest he should be shot by a savage with a poisoned arrow from behind a tree" (*SA*, 18). Like Bevis and his friend Mark, the characters can hold the two worlds together quite easily. When Captain Nancy ponders on the battle that might have been, she says, "If only we'd known, we'd have given you broadside

for broadside till one of us sank, even if it had made us late for lunch"
(*SA*, 119).

Ransome's use of the device of crossing over between the real and
the imaginary is helped by his range of characters. John is most ori-
ented to the "real" world. On the day after they catch sight of the
Amazon pirates and Captain Flint's houseboat is attacked, John
"woke in ordinary life. Well, he thought, one could hardly expect that
sort of thing to last, and it was almost a pity it had begun. After all,
even if there were no pirates, the island was real enough and so was
Swallow. He could do without the pirates. It was time to fetch the
milk" (*SA*, 104). A problem only really arises in *Swallowdale*, when
Titty becomes a little too involved in her fantasy, and later in the
series (notably in *Secret Water*) when Nancy, monomaniacally, re-
fuses to let go of the joke.

Narrative Technique
The most consistent and consistently striking and original feature of
Ransome's books is his control of pace. With *Swallowdale* as perhaps
the supreme example, what is important in his books is not so much
what happens as what does not happen. He is not afraid of the "dull"
day, and this may have been surprising to the contemporary audience—as it probably is to many young readers today. It takes, for
example, 113 pages of *Swallows and Amazons* before Nancy Blackett
makes her appearance in the flesh. Until then, the book has been
concerned with provisioning, exploring, setting up camp, fishing,
cooking, and swimming. Two chapters have what might now be regarded as suicidally downbeat titles—"Island Life" and "More Island
Life." But Ransome has sufficient faith in the *intrinsic* interest of his
material not to have to rely continually on the narrative urge. Finding out is excitement enough.

The burglary of Captain Flint's houseboat, then, stands out as an
anomaly. It involves one of the standard devices of children's books—
the child who is right, and the adults or siblings who disbelieve in
the face of what they would otherwise know to be likely. By Ransome's own standards, Titty's capture of the *Amazon* is incident
enough, without loud-voiced and loquacious burglars having reveal-
ing conversations conveniently in the dark—let alone the caricatured
things that they actually say: "Told you, you blamed fool. You've
blooming well smashed the blighted boat" (*SA*, 229).

Similarly, at the end of the book, Captain Flint gives Titty and
Roger a monkey and a parrot, the kind of exotic gifts so often found
in wish-fulfilling (and impractical) children's stories. But the fact
that monkey and parrot only reappear together in the fantasy novel

Missee Lee suggests that Ransome knew their place in the literary scheme of things.

Many incidental delights may also contribute to the way in which the books have been handed down through families. *Swallows and Amazons* is set precisely in August 1929 (*SA,* 121), and progressively, the books celebrate a lost world. (*The Picts and the Martyrs,* for example, published in 1943, is set in 1932). It could be argued that, in fact, Ransome pictures a world even earlier than that. As the background is progressively filled in with farmers, the policeman, the doctor, the postman, local boys, the cook, shopkeepers, fire-fighters, and so on, another dimension of interest is added. From the beginning, critics recognized the appeal to adults; the *Saturday Review of Literature,* for example, described *Swallows and Amazons* as having "both silvery present and golden retrospect."[25] Cars and telephones and crowds of people are very rare.

Similarly, the monetary values occasionally bring one up short. John and Susan go shopping in the village by the lake and buy four bottles of ginger beer (still a common English fizzy drink, rather in the manner of root beer) and *twenty yards* of rope for less than five shillings (*SA,* 99–100), about forty cents today.

These, then, are some of the elements that made *Swallows and Amazons* and its successors such influential and radical texts *for children.* In looking at the later novels set in the Lake District, we will be seeing, to some extent, variations played on established themes, a steady refining of Ransome's art. Ransome, as Trease observes, "deflected the stream of fiction into new channels,"[26] and by using the Lake District as a backbone and exploiting the cumulative virtues of the "series," he moved toward greater realism and, indeed, greater originality. In comparison with the later books, *Swallows and Amazons* is apprentice work, but its flaws are relatively minor. Ransome was doing something quite new, and at least in its major characteristics, his art is remarkably mature.

Swallowdale

At the end of *Swallows and Amazons,* Mrs. Dixon collects the bucket in which she brought the porridge and says:

> "Well, I suppose I shan't be seeing any of you in the morning. I shall quite miss it. . . . But perhaps you'll be coming again next year."
> "Every year. For ever and ever," said Titty.

"Aye," said Mrs. Dixon, "we all think that when we're young." (*SA*, 364)

Swallowdale (1931) is the immediate sequel to *Swallows and Amazons*. "A whole year had gone by" (*S*, 18), even though, when the Swallows meet Captain Flint, the narrator observes, "They had not seen him since the Christmas holidays and the making up of the story in the cabin of the wherry" (*S*, 96). (*Peter Duck* was half finished when *Swallowdale* came out.) Unfortunately for the fictional chronology the year is not 1930, as it should be, but 1931 (*S*, 339).

Swallowdale is, without doubt, the calmest, least plotted, and most episodic of the books; indeed, it can hardly be said to have a plot at all. True, the Swallows are dramatically shipwrecked, and the Amazons have to evade Great Aunt Maria, but apart from that, there are camping, climbing, and fishing, and little more. Ransome even includes holiday tasks—in Titty's case, learning French verbs.

With little long-term narrative thrust, *Swallowdale* relies even more than *Swallows and Amazons* on the inherent value of its material; Ransome took the bold step of allowing the thematic to take precedence over the narrative. Episodes only elaborate the theme; they rarely push the "plot" onwards. In this respect, *Swallowdale* is the most experimental of all the books: it is difficult to think of another book like it in children's literature.

Its major theme is the integration of the children into the Lake Country. While in the foreground they set up camp, shape a new mast for *Swallow*, learn to catch trout, and otherwise refine their skills, always they are aware of the countryside, and increasingly part of it. Mrs. Walker is much less in evidence, and although Captain Flint appears very regularly as general factotum and boat-repairer ex machina, the emphasis is much more on the real people of the farms, boatyards, and fells. Only the Great Aunt is excluded from this society (but, as we shall see in *The Picts and the Martyrs*, we should not jump to conclusions).

From the beginning, the pace is gentle; the return to the island, setting up camp, a visit from mother and Bridget, and the visit to Dixon's farm promise much the same mixture as before. Mrs. Dixon, especially, introduces the theme of friendly adults through her reticent husband, and she acts as an important link with the previous book.

She went back into the kitchen, and the explorers outside. could hear her say, "Go on now. There's nowt to be feared of. They're nobbut childer." And then there was the noise of iron-shod boots scraping on the slate floor, and Mr. Dixon came to the doorway wiping his mouth with the back of his hand.

"It bids fair to be a grand day," he said.

"How do you do?" said the explorers.

"Champion," said Mr. Dixon, "and—and I'm right glad to see you." He went back into the kitchen.

"He means that," said Mrs. Dixon. . . . "Dixon never was a one for talking." (*S*, 47)

All the elements cohere from the beginning. The able seaman (Titty) and the ship's boy (Roger), exploring upstream from Horseshoe Cove, see the timber-tug with its horses and red wheels go by (*S*, 58). The tug, which later passes again "in a towering wave of noise" (*S*, 287), belongs to Jack, the boyfriend of Mary Swainson (she of the clogs and butter-churn), and it is he who gives Titty a ride back to the camp on the "high-tilted end of the great log" (*S*, 404) at the end of the book. The real world now involves the children.

Ransome spent many summers as a child at Swainson's farm at Nibthwaite, where there was a watchtower rock and a "knickerbockerbreaker," both of which feature in *Swallowdale*, although the real darner of broken knickerbockers, Annie Swainson, is transformed into the fictional Mary.[27] (As the narrator observes, "You could always be sure of Mary" [*S*, 194]). It is therefore reasonable to assume that the very striking portrait of the ninety-year-old Mr. Swainson sitting in his "low-beamed farm kitchen" beside his fire ("though it was a hot day outside" [*S*, 123]) is as much reportage as invention. The description of the farm kitchen is in Ransome's best manner, suggesting both acute and genuine observation and real affection and respect. Perhaps needless to say, the observer's eyes belong to Titty:

There was a grandfather clock in the corner with a moon showing in the circle at the top, and a wreath of flowers all round the clock face. Then there was a curled hunting horn on the black chimney shelf, and above that, on pegs jutting out from the wall, an old gun, and a very long coach horn, nearly as long as a man. There were white lace curtains to the low windows, and in the deep window-seats there were fuscias in pots, and big spotted shells. Each shell had its own thick knitted mat, and the pots were in saucers, and each saucer had its knitted mat, just as if it were a spotted shell. (*S*, 124)

Roger makes a particular friend of old Mr. Swainson, who is an inveterate singer of the old ballads; but, as the old man says to John while watching him write a letter, "Eh, but you can make that pencil move. . . . And there's me. Can't write at all. Never wrote a letter these fifty years" (*S*, 272). The intimacy of the whole society is emphasized by the fact that the cook at Beckfoot is second cousin to Jack's sister-in-law (*S*, 251). Similarly, Ransome allows more insight into adult life, and when Mary Swainson banters with Jack: "'You'd think those lads had nothing else to do,' said Mary, looking after them, 'loitering about.' But she waved her hand as they passed out of sight" (*S*, 404).

Some depth is added to Nancy's character as Ransome allows her to become quite lyrical about the country activities of the Lake District, and she tells them about the hound-trails and the sheep-dog trials until "the missed meals at Beckfoot, the great-aunt, and everything else was forgotten" (*S*, 228).

The Great Aunt cannot stand against such a detailed background. When the children escape from her and climb Kanchenjunga, they meet, for a single scene, Jacky (later to star in *The Picts and the Martyrs*), who talks about the foxes taking "eight lambs . . . and eighteen fat pullets" (*S*, 316). The identification of the local people with the children is emphasized by their generally speaking to them directly, without adult interlocutors. Roger, for example, left behind in the wood with the charcoal-burners, who are part of the eternal landscape, listens to an account of wrestling. "Roger did not say that he did not understand. He just listened and the words went over his head like great poetry" (*SA*, 376).

This sense of identity among old, young, and place is also found in family matters. When Titty finds that her cave ("Peter Duck's" cave) in Swallowdale was played in by the young Captain Flint and his imaginary companion, Ben Gunn, she complains, "Had all the discoveries in the world been made already?" (*S*, 169). But the bracketing of the two imaginary characters is symbolic of both family and fictional continuity.

The same connection occurs at the cairn on the top of "Kanchenjunga" (the children's name for the mountain called "The Old Man of Coniston") when they find a message written thirty years before by Captain Flint, Mrs. Blackett, and the Amazons' father: "We climbed the Matterhorn" (*S*, 339). In this very touching moment, when nobody knows what to say, the book seems to make many nonnarrative links. "'I wonder how mother and Uncle Jim escaped from the great-aunt. . . . She was looking after them, you know.' 'Probably father rescued them'" (*S*, 339).

Swallowdale may seem to be endlessly discursive, but often past and present, family and landscape, literature and imagination are joined together—and very often in the service of the narrative. In this instance, as the children look out to sea, wondering whether, thirty years ago, the explorers could see the Isle of Man, they see the first sign of the fog that dominates much of the rest of the book. Similarly, minor explorations are given more depth by the fact that the Amazons have done things "before"; that is, a complete world exists. Thus Nancy gets blood on her hands when they shoot the bridge on the Amazon River, and comments, "I usually do"; they have to be careful about mooring the rowboat near the falls in case it swings round: "She did once, and got swamped" (*S*, 306).

The literary references and the children's fantasy lives are a continuing feature: apart from "Casabianca," which most middle-class children of that generation knew, Titty has clearly read Macaulay's "The Armada," and Roger, lying in the charcoal-burners' wigwam, imagines himself as Long John Silver.

Titty's imagination creates the old sailor, Peter Duck ("Dolls meant nothing to Titty" [*S*, 64]), although there is at times a tinge of loneliness in her romances: "There was a good deal she would have liked to say to Peter Duck himself, if only he had not happened to be out at the time" (*S*, 276). But she is pragmatic enough to wish that he were real enough to help her over a wall (*S*, 344).

Central to the book is the unheard (except by report) and only distantly seen Great Aunt. (This is one of Ransome's most accomplished narrative strategies; the prime mover remains offstage). Although perhaps a little dated, even in 1930 or 1931, she certainly serves to polarize all Ransome's themes of freedom and locality: the housemaid, another domestic in the middle-class world, is seen dancing when the "G.A." leaves (*S*, 327).

The Great Aunt disapproves of virtually everything; Roger is amazed that she should not like daisies on lawns (*S*, 299). Titty thinks of her as a Gorgon, turning Nancy and Peggy into stone figures of smart and respectable little girls: "I don't believe even Captain Flint felt properly springy while she was anywhere near" (*S*, 345). This "prim, elderly lady" (*S*, 165) commits the cardinal sin in both family codes: she makes a mother (Mrs. Blackett) cry. "Titty stared [at Nancy] and her mouth stayed open. She tried to think what she would do if anybody ever tried to make the best of all natives cry. 'It was about us, of course' [said Nancy]. 'She dragged father in. We know because after we'd gone to bed we couldn't help hearing Uncle Jim talking to mother just outside our window, and he said, "Bob would have liked them as they are." And he called mother "Mops," which he only does sometimes. Then we made a noise and mother said, "Go to sleep, you donkeys," and pretended to laugh. But she couldn't.' Nancy walked suddenly away, but she came back in a moment with her face very red" (*S*, 223–24).

To balance this, she does provide moments of humor, as when she catches her great-nieces pretending that she is a heathen goddess and bowing before her window in the middle of the night; and she cements the bond between the children and the sympathetic adults, such as Captain Flint: "Now then, I haven't seen your allies and I'd rather not, but just you tell them from me, if you *should* happen to meet them, that if they want to signal right bang in the middle of the day, it wouldn't be so hard on their friends if they'd chose blackbirds or jays instead of owls. Your Aunt Maria wants to write to the Natural History Museum about it" (*S*, 297).

Many of the themes and patterns of *Swallows and Amazons* are revisited. Adult reinforcement occurs after each troublesome incident: mother arrives to reassure Titty over the voodoo doll; Captain Flint arrives to help with the repair of the wrecked *Swallow*. Swallowdale itself is made safe because, with the telescope, they can see Holly Howe, across the lake (*S*, 162).

But, as before, codes and skills quietly dominate the foreground. John *must* raise *Swallow* from the lakebed; it is a point of honor. He refers, as before, to his father ("'I wonder if it ever happened to daddy. I don't suppose it ever did, though'" [*S*, 117]). And there is great pleasure in descriptions of how to make a heather broom, how to plane and oil a mast, how to light a fire (again) without paper, how to navigate using a compass, or how to cook corned beef ("This gives the meat just that touch of camp-fire smoke that makes the difference" [*S*, 236]). The moral lesson of rowing round and round an island in the fog is as important as any potential excitement involved.

Character development is on much the same lines. Each is allowed more foregrounding, and only in the case of Susan does the monomania become not only a little tiresome, but also authorially endorsed. It seems that, for once, Ransome is writing for parents as well as for children. Susan worries to the point of fatalism—"'We're here, anyway,' she said. 'So even if it's all wrong it can't be helped now'"— but Ransome seems to feel that any annoyance felt by child readers has to be deflected: "Really, if it had not been for Susan, half the Swallows' adventures would have been impossible, but, with a mate as good as that, to see that everything went as it should, there was no need of any native to worry about what was happening" (*S*, 321, 325).

The relationship between the Swallows and Amazons is still occasionally uneasy ("There was something about these Amazons hard for them to understand" [*S*, 307]). The collusion of Mrs. Blackett and Captain Flint in Nancy and Peggy's misbehavior is *not* the way things are done in the Walker family, and it adds a certain irony to the Great Aunt's having the temerity to visit to "inspect" Mrs. Walker.

Swallowdale is also distinguished by its painting of scenery. Ransome takes time to describe the sun coming up on Kanchenjunga and slowly moving down the mountain until the children awake; the swans flying out over the hills; and the view from "the roof of the world": "Far, far away, beyond range after range of low hills, the land ended and the sea began, the real sea, the blue water stretching on and on until it met the sky" (*S*, 335). This passage reads like an unconscious (or conscious) echo of Wordsworth on Snowdon in *The Prelude:*

> Far, far beyond, the vapours shot themselves,
> In headlands, tongues, and promontory shapes,
> Into the Sea, the real Sea, that seemed
> To dwindle and give up its majesty.[28]

Swallowdale is a book of milk fresh from the cow, of Titty repeating the word *watershed* "as if she had been waiting for [it]" (*S*, 410), and of Ransome's long and lyrical description not only of trout fishing, but of trout flies. Captain Flint, who "of course" ties his own flies and "was impatient himself to be fishing" (*S*, 197–98), is Ransome walking the pages of his own book. He also walks it in his alter ego, John, who considers the look of Swallowdale without tents: "It did not look like anybody's home, and John knew that when they had gone back to Wild Cat island, Swallowdale would look as if they had never been there. . . . Everything would be as it had been, and their own Swallowdale, with its neat tents and cheerful fire, would do no more than a memory or something he had read about in a book. It was a queer thought, not comfortable" (*S*, 274).

Such questions of youth, size, space, and immortality that spring out of such a radically organized book as *Swallowdale* are perhaps ones that require a philosopher of a less pragmatic turn of mind— the kind of philosopher who appears as another of Ransome's other selves in the next Lake District book, set only a few months away.

Winter Holiday

Dick Callum is the son of an academic, given to wiping his glasses in moments of stress and utterly, simplistically practical. Dorothea Callum is constantly romancing, and endlessly not finishing her stories.

Together they provide a curious composite self-portrait of Ransome
and give rise to a splendidly lyrical passage.

As Dorothea thinks, Dick "sometimes, in some queer way of his
own . . . seemed to hit on things that made stories and real life come
closer together than usual."[29] Standing in the winter landscape of the
Lake District, Dick, currently an astronomer, looks up at the sky:

> Those little stars that seemed to speckle a not too dreadfully
> distant blue ceiling were farther away than he could make
> himself think, try as he might. . . . He felt for a moment less
> than nothing, and then, suddenly, size did not seem to mat-
> ter. Distant and huge the stars might be, but he, standing
> there with chattering teeth on the dark hillside, could see
> them and name them and even foretell what next they were
> going to do. . . . He felt an odd wish to shout at them in
> triumph, but remembered in time that this would not be sci-
> entific. (WH, 34)

The strengths of *Winter Holiday* (1933) are the contrast between
the established characters and the new characters and the evocation
of the snowy landscape and the frozen lake. Its great weakness is the
mechanistic plot of its last third, with heavy reliance on the contriv-
ances of Captain Flint and rather irresponsible (for Ransome) deviation from proportion and good sense.

In *Winter Holiday,* Ransome took a considerable risk: he allowed
his established characters to be viewed through the eyes of others. It
has to be said that they do not come off very well.

The eyes belong to Dick and Dorothea, who are given their creden-
tials by Mr. and Mrs. Dixon; continuity from *Swallowdale* is main-
tained by the farmer's shyness ("He's not one for talking, isn't Dixon"
[WH, 18]). Dick's rescue of the cragfast sheep allows a pleasant variation upon this theme: it brings "a queer kind of alliance between
Dick and Mr. Dixon. They were neither of them great talkers, but
together they got along very well" (WH, 161). Mr. Dixon, with his
extravagances of speech ("He went so far as to say 'Champion,' and
'I'm right glad of that'" [WH, 173]) and his rivalry with the Jacksons,
gives the Callums a status within the community that even the Swallows and Amazons lack. Mr. Dixon surprises even his wife: "And after
breakfast, for the first time since they had known him, [he] spoke
first without being spoken to. 'Happen you'd be liking to come with
me to the smithy whiles we get runners fixed and all trig?' Mrs.
Dixon looked at him in astonishment" (WH, 160).

Dorothea, similarly, is not a total outsider ("The very spit of your
mother," as Mrs. Dixon says [WH, 159]) but there is an excellent mo-

ment at the outset when Dorothea first sees the Swallows and Amazons and potential pathos is catapulted into bathos by her romanticising: "She had been very happy, waking up in this new place, but those children in the boat had somehow spoilt things. What fun they were having, six of them, all together. A story began to shape itself in her mind, one that no-body would be able to read without tears. . . . *The Outcasts*. By Dorothea Callum. Chapter I. 'The two children, brother and sister, shared their last few crumbs and looked this way and that along the deserted shore. Was this to be the end?' 'Oh well,' said Dick. 'We can't help not having a boat'" (*WH*, 24).

How far Ransome intends his "senior" characters to appear patronizing toward the D.'s is not clear. John is rather priggish, Roger is rude, and they have an unfortunate consciousness of their own superiority ("But what's *she* going to do?" [*WH*, 51]). Titty, on the other hand, is kind, and Susan pragmatic—"It would be rather beastly to leave them out of things" (*WH*, 60)—although Susan, in a memorably Wordsworthian line, and despite several weeks' acquaintance with the D.'s, says uncharitably, "If only they had any sense. . . . But they haven't not got any, not that sort. People oughtn't to be allowed to be brought up in towns" (*WH*, 332). This unsympathetic remark calls to mind Ransome's rage at caravan sites in the Lake District; perhaps this is a revelation of the unacceptable face of the exclusive society.

Fortunately, the D.'s are resilient, for they have an initiation that lasts for the whole book. Although they prove themselves to some extent by their skating, even at the very end of the book, the assumption is made that it is the D.'s who are at fault: "Presently Nancy noticed that John, Susan, and Peggy, although they had come to rescue them, had very little to say to the D.'s" (*WH*, 351).

One problem for the Callums is that their codes are less developed. Small matters such as being able to light a fire are elevated to major proportions ("'Newspaper?' Susan and Peggy were staring at her. 'Newspaper! For lighting a fire!' . . . 'You'd better come along with us at once,' said Nancy, 'and see how to make a fire and how to light it with one match and no paper at all'" [*WH*, 48]); worse, they do not (at first) understand the fascination with sailing and the ice-yacht (*WH*, 192) or the fact that "rowing boats don't count" (*WH*, 95).

But the judicious reader might be inclined to give them some sympathy. Although their relationship is not shown to any depth at this stage, they do at least understand each other's lesser foibles. When Dick is giving himself a lecture on centers of gravity during his attempt to rescue the cragfast sheep, Titty says, "I suppose he's all right?" and Dorothea replies, "Quite . . . so long as he talks like that" (*WH*, 143). Similarly, although Dick often regards his sister with incomprehension, he is prepared to be charitable. When she is trying to get a sense of what it must be like to be in charge of the houseboat, she puts the ladder up so that she can take it down again. "Dick said nothing. If Dorothea wanted a thing, he supposed there was some sense in it, though he could not see it at the moment" (*WH,* 237).

Dorothea's character (like Peggy's) is limited by the necessity that everyone be a little slow on the uptake when compared with Nancy and the reader. Also, her storytelling talents seem slightly improbable—*could* she keep the others enthralled for hours on end? But at least she has good taste: she has, for example, read *Old Peter's Russian Tales,* for where else would she have heard of "the little girl who sat on her wedding chest in the winter forest, waiting for the coming of Frost" (*WH,* 79)?

The most telling statement about Dorothea comes when she meets Captain Flint, who arrives home to his houseboat to find it occupied by strangers: "He looked at Dorothea in great astonishment. He was not angry. Nobody ever was angry with Dorothea" (*WH,* 248). (The doctor in *The Picts and the Martyrs* has a similar reaction [*PM,* 86]).

In the clashes of family codes, the D.'s offer the child reader another perspective. Dorothea listens "with grave interest" when Peggy attacks Captain Flint: "It seemed to her a queer way of talking to an uncle, though, as she and Dick had no uncles of their own, she had no personal experience of dealing with them" (*WH,* 269).

The new perspective disguises the weakness of the plotting. In no other book (except perhaps *Secret Water*) is there such a sense of the children acting out something contrived and allowed for by the adults. In contrast with the episodic and thematically structured *Swallowdale, Winter Holiday* is so plot-based that Ransome loses his balance. Some of the most gripping episodes, such as Dick and the cragfast sheep, are based on an improbability—in that case, separation of the two groups of children on the dangerous snowy fells. Even when things go wrong and the children are apparently lost in a blizzard, he emphasizes not the danger, but the excitement. In short, he makes it too easy: the police and the search parties are "stirred up" and then dismissed; "dinners had rather a tendency to turn into feasts" (*WH,* 358, 273). Even the brilliantly paced climax requires the D.'s to skate past the occupied houseboat, and Ransome is forced to insert a short history of the "North Pole" to explain events.

But *Winter Holiday* has many compensations, such as the innovative pacing that produces a tension-slackening chapter title such as "Next Morning," or the view of Captain Flint through the eyes of Mrs. Dixon, "who had known Captain Flint when he was a boy, [and who] said that growing older and travelling round the world brought no sense to some folk" (*WH,* 273).

Whatever its shortcomings, *Winter Holiday* can be treasured for the addition of more local and period details. The beds are warmed by hot bricks wrapped in flannel (*WH*, 156); the farmhand Silas's accent is pure Lake District ("It's not sic a job as we can't tackle it" [*WH*, 156]); jugs of water stand in the bedrooms for washing. References are made to the great frost of 1895: "It'll never be what it was . . . in '95, with coaches with four horses and horns blowing crossing the lake from side to side" (*WH*, 188), and Mrs. Blackett reminisces of the hot-pot that sank through the ice "when I was young, and the lake was frozen all over" (*WH*, 87). The perch that Dick sees, frozen in the ice "as if it were swimming in glass" (*WH*, 165) comes directly from life: Ransome wrote in the *Autobiography*, "I saw a perch frozen in the ice, preserved as if in glass beneath my feet" (*A*, 48).

Then there are descriptions of the shippen and the smithy, where the smith is happy to make sleds—"That means work enough, and welcome these days with no horses left but on the farms" (*WH*, 162)— and Sammy the policeman (from *Swallows and Amazons*) trying the ice. The laconic doctor ("The car's meant to hold four, so there ought to be room for a mere eight" [*WH*, 107]); the invisible Fanny who helps Mrs. Jackson (*WH*, 173); the Jackson's dog Ringman; Sammy's mother, Mrs. Lewthwaite (*WH*, 311); and the man selling hot pies for two pence (about eight cents today) all round out the picture (*WH*, 289). Even the revelation that Roger wears a collar-stud (*WH*, 262)— which he picks with his teeth out of the washbasin to practice diving—should remind us that this is indeed a different world.

Above all, *Winter Holiday* creates the atmosphere of the long winter, the polished ice, and the snow on the hills, through the eyes of an "outsider" who mediates between the average reader and the privileged place: "And then there was this magical brightness in the air. At home, in the town, Dorothea had seen snow more than once, where it lay for a few hours in the streets, growing grimier from the smoke, until it was swept into dirty heaps along the gutters. She has [*sic*] never seen anything like this" (*WH*, 77).

Pigeon Post

Pigeon Post (1936) is Ransome at the top of his form as a narrator. Dedicated to Oscar Gnospellius, the mining-engineer husband of Barbara Collingwood (and thus uncle by marriage to the Altounyan–Swallows), it won the first Carnegie Medal. In this connection, Marcus Crouch suggests that the award may have been as much for past achievement as for the book itself; *Pigeon Post,* "if not Ransome's best book, was rich in the qualities which distinguished all his work."[30]

But the book is far better than Crouch suggests. Not only is it the most intricately constructed of Ransome's novels, with the most sustained forward thrust, but if one were to look for an example of Ransome as pure structural craftsman, then one would choose the opening chapters of this book.

In a very significant scene, during one of those quiet intervals in the action that Ransome copes with so well, Titty sits and listens to Dorothea's new story: "The afternoon slipped by in literary criticism. No novelist ever had a happier audience. 'It's a simply splendid story,' said Titty, when Dorothea had read to the end of her notebooks, and explained what was still to come, and had gone back to the first chapter to remind Titty of the little bits that were going to be important later on."[31]

Pigeon Post is a very rich book in terms of narrative events, but Ransome contrives to prefigure almost everything (as well as to provide a retrospect) at the outset. Roger and Titty's train journey from the junction to "Rio" brings in, from the second sentence, Roger's character marker of the chocolate; and soon mentions the pigeons, the Blacketts and the Callums, the reason that the children are not immediately sailing, and even the climax. As the farmer's wife—who is symbolic of the other local characters who are to appear—says, "And where there's no engines there's visitors with motor-cars and matches and cigarettes and no more thought in their heads than a cheese has. It takes nobbut a spark to start a fire when all's bone dry for the kindling" (*PP,* 16).

We are introduced to the structural device of the running joke. Captain Flint has sent an enigmatic telegram saying "BE KIND TO TIMOTHY GIVE HIM THE RUN OF MY ROOM" (*PP,* 28). Dick decides that Timothy is probably an armadillo, and the children build it a hutch. Only in the penultimate chapter is Timothy revealed to be Captain Flint's shy partner, the rival prospector with the squashy hat.

Similarly, they pass Colonel Jolys in his car with his hunting horn, used to rally the firefighters; they reminisce about the last holiday and the ice, meet "Rattletrap" and Mrs. Blackett, and wait on the pier for the action to begin, with Titty thinking of two years before, when she first saw "the little white sail of the Amazon pirates" (*PP,* 21). This comprehensive foreshadowing, without a single word of direct authorial intervention, is a remarkable demonstration of the craft of fiction.

Chapter 2 simply backs up this technique and introduces the new theme, mining. From then on—excepting the famous Ransome lulls—the plot sprints forward, each element logically and sequentially linked. There are no isolated incidents, no divergences. Unlike its predecessors, *Pigeon Post* is a book of unified plot, and the pace seems to accelerate toward its ending.

Moreover, the plot is far from implausible. In fact, with regard to the behavior of the adult characters and the relationship of the characters to the landscape, it is probably the most plausible of all (if we accept, as we well may, Timothy's shyness: "But why, why, didn't you go straight to Beckfoot?" "My dear Jim, how could I? There were children popping up all over the place. It was like a school feast" [*PP*, 383]).

If, in *Winter Holiday,* the implicit indulgence of the children by adults was made explicit, in *Pigeon Post* there is no such pandering, with the result that the book gains considerably in apparent reality, and exciting incidents become the more plausible. Mrs. Blackett, serving cold mutton in a house full of painters, dashing round homicidally in what we have to remember was a very rare object in the Lake District, her battered car "Rattletrap" (also taken from life—the "perambulating biscuit tin" of Low Ludderburn[32]), is seen as a not quite responsible adult. She is a genuine, slightly harassed mother who, through her own lack of discipline, is outgeneralled by her children:

> "They haven't *gone*?" said Mrs. Blackett. "I did want to see Nancy. I've been thinking over that idea of your all going up on the fells to camp. There was something I wanted to say to her."
> "She was afraid there might be," said Roger.
> Mrs. Blackett's mouth opened. For a moment nothing came out of it. . . .
> "My own fault," she said. "I ought to have got up in the middle of the night to make sure of that dreadful girl." (*PP*, 59)

This is about the extent of her censure of her daughters.

She has a structural role as well, placing obstacles in the children's way, but like most of Ransome's adults, she is really on their side ("Send out your pioneers" [*PP*, 55]). She even buttresses Susan's self-image: "'I put all my trust in you, Susan,' said Mrs. Blackett. 'And you too, John,' she added. John grinned. It was kind of her to say it, but he knew she did not mean it. On questions of milk and drinking-water and getting able-seamen to bed in proper time, Susan was the one the natives trusted" (*PP*, 55).

The same cannot be said for the redoubtable Mrs. Tyson. She is not impressed by Nancy, and an adult—indeed, a child with growing responsibility—might be forgiven for sympathizing with her deep suspicions. As (despite Ransome's disclaimer), one of the lower orders, Mrs. Tyson provides food and her orchard for the explorers, and "meant it all so kindly that even Nancy could not say no to her" (*PP*, 103). When the prospectors are late for her meals, it is difficult to know with whom to sympathize. Thus Mrs. Tyson achieves three-dimensional status, even if her visit to the camp is a trifle melodramatically timed. She is "frightened and angry" at the blast furnace. Nancy tries to reassure her—"We'll be done by to-morrow"—and receives a tart reply: "You'll be home to-morrow and away out of here. . . . Have you all gone daft?" (*PP*, 320). She also casts herself as villain by committing the cardinal sin (toward Susan, the mother surrogate). She accuses them (not unreasonably) of starting the fire: "A moment before, Susan's face had been all thankfulness that nobody was burnt. But now she too had heard what Mrs. Tyson had said. Titty felt tears starting in her own eyes. Nothing ought ever to happen to make Susan look like that" (*PP*, 370).

Very typical of Ransome's sense of balance is Mrs. Tyson's subsequent apology, which is brief, low-key, and tied into the background of work and reality that stabilizes all the books: "'But you mun forgive me. When a fire's afoot a body can't think. And if you'd not been here with they pigeons, we'd have had our farms burnt, and the hay in t' fields and all, before anybody could have gotten word. So I thank you. . . . Now then, Robin. Nowt to stare at. We've the cows to milk, fire or no fire. And late it is and all.' And Mrs. Tyson and Robin and the farm hand went down into the wood. 'So that's all right,' said Mrs. Blackett" (*PP*, 375).

Similarly, Slater Bob, despite his family connection with the Blacketts ("Mind ye, yer mother's father took me wi' him when he went to Africa after that same stuff" [*PP*, 42]), only plays games so far. Once he has talked to Timothy, he becomes pragmatically unsympathetic to Nancy's games: "Aw reet for t' likes o' him. Why, he's a miner. . . . Why, he's as good a miner as I am. . . . You can tell Miss Nancy from me she should know better than to let you folk into t' levels. . . . Nay, there's nowt wrong wi' his hat. . . . And the mining that man's done, it's a pleasure to hear him" (*PP*, 261–62).

Captain Flint, perhaps by dint of his comparative unimportance here, becomes part of the believable background. His character is even reinforced by the period detail; he has, for example, to dictate the telephone number of the firefighters at the moment of crisis: "Fellside, seven five. . . . No. . . . Not nine. . . . FIVE. . . . F for Fool. I for idiot . . . Yes . . . SEVEN FIVE" (*PP*, 366).

If the adults, then, are realistic, what of the children? Dick and Titty take some steps toward maturity. Titty's long struggle with herself to learn to dowse, and to put herself through an upsetting experience, is not as extreme as her experiments with the wax voodoo doll in *Swallowdale.* As Margery Fisher says, "Her struggle to force herself to try again in private . . . is a key to her character."[33] That she positively looks forward to trying again, and that in the end she measures her achievement by its contribution not to the game but to the long-term effect on the animals who will drink from the spring, marks a significant step forward.

But the book really belongs to Dick. The studious outsider makes the pigeons ring the bell and organizes the smelting of the "gold": in a sense, he represents an alternative to the romantics, the tomboys, and the career-oriented proto-adults who surround him. Refreshingly, he doesn't really register Nancy's games. When they are caught inspecting Squashy Hat's ore samples on the Topps, Nancy hurriedly puts down the paint pot, and John feels as though he's been caught in someone else's garden, whereas Dick, pragmatically, says, "Let's ask him what this stuff is" (*PP,* 190).

He is also central to what is probably Ransome's most skilled piece of narrative. Ransome had been developing the "parallel scene" narrative in his earlier books (and had used it to excellent effect, as we have seen, in *The Picts and the Martyrs*), but it reaches its apotheosis in *Pigeon Post.* Dick cycles away toward Beckfoot in a last attempt to analyze the ore sample. The older children are in the mine; the younger children are asleep in their tents. A careless visitor starts a fell fire with a cigarette. First we see the frantic attempts of the younger children to contain the fire, then the older children surrounded by fire—and then we return to the rather bewildered figure of Dick, arriving at the quiet and calm of Beckfoot. Although the audience is avidly awaiting the denouement, and although Dick himself is desperate to get his analysis done, he "found himself somehow in the dining-room eating cold beef and salad" (*PP,* 357). The adult world is unaware of the children's games, but it is also unaware of the seriousness of the situation.

The arrival of the pigeon with the warning message is as satisfying a galvanization into action as could be wished, and, unlike *Winter Holiday,* the children and the adults assume their realistic and unsentimental places in the scheme of things. What the children do retain, though, is their dignity.

Underlying the drama are the established themes of family, work, and place. When Roger stays out late and the other children are getting extremely worried and start to plan search parties, the reaction when he eventually arrives is suitably natural: "Pity and fear for him

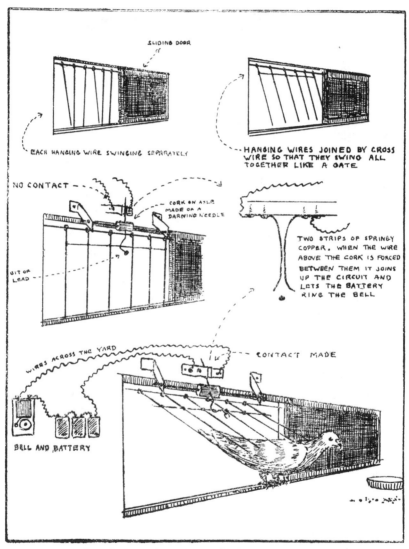

HOW DICK MADE THE PIGEONS RING A BELL

were gone in a moment. 'Miserable little idiot,' said John" (*PP,* 209). Beyond family is the code of hard work with no easy shortcuts. Prospecting is dull, things have to be earned and achieved. And beyond that is the love and sense of place. These cohere, because those who truly belong to the Lake District (by birth or in spirit) save it by traditional methods (pigeons, firebrooms, water from a well found by dowsing) from destruction by fire caused by outsiders.

For its narrative integrity, unity of purpose, and the many skills it celebrates, *Pigeon Post* must count among the best of the series—as, indeed, must its successor in the Lake District books, the last of the sequence.

The Picts and the Martyrs

Between *Pigeon Post* and *The Picts and the Martyrs* (1943), a great deal has happened to the characters who appear in the latter—and, indeed, to those who do not. Dick and Dorothea, for this is really their book, have consolidated their characters, as well as their maritime skills, in *The Big Six.* Nancy and Peggy have continued to play games, albeit a trifle uneasily, in *Secret Water.* And, perhaps most significantly, the Walkers have undergone a sea-change in *We Didn't Mean to Go to Sea,* with the result that they are, as it were, a family apart when it comes to *Secret Water. The Picts and the Martyrs* is, in effect, the coda, pushing the characterizations of Nancy and Peggy as far as they can go in relationship with their friends, given their secondary place in Ransome's narrative world. After this book, far from "five whole weeks of the holidays still to go" (*PM,* 303), the holidays are actually over.

Thus *The Picts and the Martyrs* is a highly atmospheric book. Although far from autumnal—indeed, Dick and Dorothea survive without windows for more than a week and remain warm (an unlikely circumstance in most contemporary English summers)—the atmosphere (literally and metaphorically) is heavy with water: rain, the lake, the becks.

The sympathy is, as it is not in any of the other books, entirely with the learners, who survive by their own good wits. The book has a very characteristic ending, with multilayered action that is second or equal to that of *Pigeon Post.* The use of background characters in the Lake District is the most developed; as the fifth book in this setting, and the eleventh of the series, we are entering a complete, rounded world.

One attraction of *The Picts and the Martyrs* lies in the acceptance by the adult world of the Callums, without patronization. Dick and

Dorothea, in their hut in the woods, meet, as it were, the "real" society, unmediated by Nancy and Peggy. Another is the idea of the children apart, but still secure; and then there is the way in which the children are actually protecting the adults (Mrs. Blackett and Captain Flint) from Great Aunt Maria. Finally comes the revelation that Aunt Maria can be, and is, as unsure of herself as the next person; she grows from a caricature to a real human being. As Timothy, another cipher who becomes three-dimensional, remarks, "If you ask me, I think your Great Aunt is remarkably like her Great Niece" (*PM*, 301).

The shortest of the novels, *The Picts and the Martyrs* builds on the earlier ones. Mary Swainson and Jacky reappear from *Swallowdale*, Timothy and Colonel Jolys and Slater Bob from *Pigeon Post*, Cook and Sammy the policeman from *Swallows and Amazons*, and the laconic doctor from *Winter Holiday*. Even the boat-builder from *Swallowdale* makes an appearance, as we have seen, and has to cope with Ransome's immortal views on boat-builders in general.

The children are entering the adult world, and Dick and Dorothea (if not Nancy) are open to new areas of irony. When the doctor says to Nancy, "I wish you were at the bottom of the deep blue sea," Dick remarks, a trifle innocently: "'Timothy said something like that . . . A message. He said we were to tell you that he knew somebody who'd like to wring your neck. He meant he would, but he didn't say why.' 'Natives are all alike,' said Nancy. 'But it doesn't matter.'" (*PM*, 82–83).

Skills are as much emphasized, but on two planes. The D.'s now have their own boat, and they wish to learn how to use it without the superiority of Nancy and Peggy impinging on them. The result is that Nancy and Peggy are relegated to rather more shadowy positions—which is just as well, considering that Ransome allows Nancy (without perceptible irony) to voice such incomprehensible advice as "never forget to mouse the sister-hooks when you fasten the main halliard to the yard." No wonder "Dick's mind was in a whirl" (*PM*, 141).

If Dick becomes a real boat owner, struggling with the intricacies of sailing, so Dorothea becomes at least a willing housekeeper. Even the omniscient Susan has not been shown dealing with a rabbit: as Dorothea says, "It looks awfully dead." Dick's scientific reply, "But it *is* dead," does not help (*PM*, 134). This is perhaps the measure of *The Picts and the Martyrs*; Ransome is now writing not about play, but about reality:

> "In the cookery book," she said, "the rabbits and things all seem to be born naked and ready for cooking. . . ."

> Dick took the rabbit by its hind legs and went out.
> Dorothea read feverishly in the cookery book. Minute after
> minute passed. Dick came back. He was looking very green.
> "Dick?" said Dorothea, and he knew it was a question.
> "No, I wasn't. . . . But very nearly. . . . Things inside it . . ."
> "I'm a pig, Dick," said Dorothea. "I oughtn't to have let you
> do it all by yourself. . . ."
> No one who has not tried to take it off can know how
> firmly a rabbit's skin sticks to a rabbit. . . . It was a messy
> business but so difficult that after the first few moments
> Dorothea forgot its messiness, and clawed and tugged at
> skin and body as if nothing mattered in the world except to
> get them apart. (*PM,* 170, 171)

This highly significant passage demonstrates the metamorphosis of
Dorothea and Dick into children with experiences that go beyond
those of their mentors.

As part of the D.'s' education, the local boy, Jacky, is very important. He is, in his laconic way, the epitome of the Lake District people. Rabbits need only an onion to cook with them; trout can be
"guddled" with ease (although, for anyone who has lain by a trout
stream, Dick and Dorothea catch them just a little too easily). And
so Ransome is taking Jacky quite seriously when he says, "'Summer
and back end's our busy time . . .' as if he owned a thousand acres.
'Aye busiest when other folk are having holidays. I'se going wi' dad
to market today. We've young pigs to sell'" (*PM,* 131).

This is a world away from Nancy and Peggy, who, although their
games are fairly serious in this instance, are still playing games.
Only toward the end of the book, when Nancy saves the Great Aunt
from embarrassment ("Their eyes met for a moment. It was surprising, but it almost seemed that the Great Aunt was pleased" [*PM,*
291]), does she seem to realize that she is dealing with a human
being. The moment soon passes, though, and Nancy, saying "Mother
will be awfully pleased" (*PM,* 301) returns to her simplistic view of
life. Dick's final words are to plan to sail down to the houseboat to
continue with the assays from the mine; Nancy's are to plan new
games that will interrupt the work.

Ransome seems, if not to have lost sympathy with Nancy and
Peggy, rather to have loaded the narrative dice against them. *The
Picts and the Martyrs* is for the Callums what *We Didn't Mean to Go
to Sea* was for the Walkers, and the Blacketts have no equivalent
maturing experience.

The theme of displacement that has gradually developed through
the series is strongest in *The Picts and the Martyrs*; the normal props

of security are removed. The adults who remain, notably the cook and
Timothy, are inadequate as parents. Timothy, interestingly, is one of
the few people that the cook *does* attempt to dominate: "You'll be
stopping for lunch, Mr. Stedding. . . . And you should NOT be lying
on that damp grass even if the sun is shining" (*PM,* 302). (Timothy
ignores her.) And so the children have to reassess their situation. In
Nancy's case this unmooring merely means a temporary interruption
to her generally egocentric progress—but again, this attitude may
well be a function of the distance at which Ransome continually
keeps her throughout the series. After all, the Walkers were heavily
influenced by, if not actually based on, real children. Dick and Dorothea come from aspects of himself. Only Nancy and Peggy are "pure"
fiction, children glimpsed on the lake (or, as Lancelyn Green senti-
mentally puts it, "slipped for an instant out of the Paradise of Fiction,
to supply the great moment of inspiration").[34] Nancy may dominate
the first scenes and have the last word, but the modest Dick and
Dorothea are central. They have been initiated at last. The combined
self-portrait, first seen in *Winter Holiday,* has joined the exclusive
society, and, indeed, upstaged some of its oldest members.

We may or may not agree with a contemporary reviewer that "the
plot . . . is a little strained";[35] like *Pigeon Post* and unlike *Swallowdale, The Picts and the Martyrs* is a plot-based book, with incidents
embedded in and contributing to the plot. (*Swallows and Amazons*
and *Winter Holiday* are hybrids in this respect.) More than in any
other book (except, perhaps, *The Big Six*) there is a tension between
the needs of a clearly articulated narrative and the fascination of the
incidental details.

The Picts and the Martyrs is a celebration—the culmination of a
celebration, of the landscape and people that Ransome loved most.
In perhaps the most accomplished chapter, one that looks forward
to Ransome's unfulfilled career as an adult novelist, "The Great
Aunt Goes to See for Herself," we see the children's world from the
outside. Through a succession of local characters—the cook, Billy
Lewthwaite, the butcher's man, and Mary Swainson—we are given a
final tour through the scenes of the earlier books. The chapter is almost a requiem.

This book shows how far Ransome and his characters have come
from the tentative explorations of this mental, moral, and actual
landscape in *Swallows and Amazons*; and it is a very fitting end to
Ransome's fictive engagement with the country of his childhood.

6

On the Norfolk Broads:
Coots and Detectives

The change of scene from the Lake District to the fen country of eastern England took Ransome to another favorite landscape. The two books *Coot Club* and *The Big Six* are set in the spring and autumn of the third fictional year (*Coot Club* immediately precedes *Pigeon Post*), and they continue the initiation of Dick and Dorothea (although *Coot Club* was planned initially with a fresh set of characters, in order to contrast town and country.)[1] This time, however, they are outsiders seen only partially from the inside: like *Pigeon Post, Coot Club* and *The Big Six* are more balanced books than their predecessors; the focus is spread more evenly between the groups of children.

The books also contribute to two different genres. *Coot Club* is essentially a cruise novel, *The Big Six* a detective novel. As in *Winter Holiday,* Dick and Dorothea are the novices, and also as in *Winter Holiday,* Dick's earnest approach to learning and Dorothea's novelette-ish view of the world provide both a motive for the passing on of much knowledge and a contrast with the world of reality.

Again, Ransome has managed to create a convincing set of characters, with their own infrastructure, in a setting that is realistic as well as symbolic and is based on his own experience. Ransome had sailed on the Broads a good deal, notably in 1931 (aboard a yacht called *Welcome*) and 1933 and in 1934 to check details and background for *Coot Club.* In 1938, Ransome and Evgenia led "a perfect fleet" with "three families whom they had met at Pin Mill" and old friends from the Lakes, Taqui and Titty Altounyan.[2]

Coot Club

In recent years, the waterways of the Norfolk Broads have suffered (rather like the Lake District) from being "loved to death," and the fish and bird life have been under attack from pollution, agricultural fertilizer, and, perhaps, too many boats. Both of these books are much concerned with the change and loss of the environment; indeed, *Coot Club* (1934) can be seen as a symbolic battle between the evil of the "Hullabaloos" on their noisy motor cruiser and the quiet life they seem, casually, to destroy. Their cruiser, the *Margoletta,* is the target, for Ransome, of a rather sustained attack.

On came the *Margoletta,* sweeping up with the tide, and filling the quiet evening with a loud treacly voice:

I want to be a darling, a doodle-um, a duckle-um,
I want to be a ducky, doodle darling, yes, I do.

"Indeed," muttered Port, with a good deal of bitterness. "Try next door," said Starboard. (*CC,* 331)

Ransome is writing of a lost period of fast sailing wherries (only a single wherry survives today) and Thames barges. *Coot Club* is almost a tour of the Broads (the places are all real, except for the occasional house), but even in the 1930s, things were changing. When, for example, Dick and Dorothea and their companions visit the old town of Beccles, they call at a shop "with a sign hanging out over the pavement. 'Hmph!' said the Admiral [Mrs. Barrable], 'it wasn't "ye olde" when I used to buy buns there, but I daresay the buns will be none the worse for it'" (*CC,* 270–71). The books can be read, even more than the Lake District books, as pieces of social history, perhaps the more so because Ransome immediately integrates the adults of the area into the book.

As with all Ransome books, *Coot Club* demonstrates a deep running ethic—almost a law, in the sense that Kipling laid out the Law of the Jungle in *The Jungle Book:* "The Law of the Jungle, which never orders anything without a reason, forbids every beast to eat Man. . . . The real reason for this is that man-killing means . . . the arrival of white men . . . with guns. . . . Then everybody in the jungle suffers. . . . The reason the beasts give among themselves is . . . it is unsportsmanlike."[3] The children of the Broads feel the same about visitors (as Susan did in *Pigeon Post*). The mainspring of the plot of *Coot Club* is that Tom Dudgeon, the local boy, breaks a basic rule, not by casting off the *Margoletta,* though that breaks an essential sailing rule, whether or not saving the Coot's nest provides an excuse; but by a more serious trespass. "'Don't get mixed up with foreigners' was the beginning and end of the law" (*CC*, 77), and the importance of this interdiction is emphasized by the immediate complicity of the adults of all classes. Both Tom's father and mother immediately forgive him for casting off the boat, and his father's attitude is distinctly ambiguous: "'It's a pity it's happened . . . and I'll be very much obliged if you can manage not to let those rowdies catch you . . . but . . . I don't really see what else you could have done'" (*CC*, 80). The point is not that Tom has done wrong, but that *he was seen.* Similarly, Jim Woodall, skipper of one of the fastest wherries, and as such a professional of immensely high standing in Ransome's (and his characters') estimation, regards Tom's actions primarily from the point of view of regional loyalty: "And if they were not to blame? Well, Jim Wooddall was Norfolk too. 'If a Norfolk boy done it,' he said to himself, 'those chaps can cover the place with paper before anyone give him away'" (*CC*, 139).

But Ransome is far too subtle a writer to allow the book to degenerate into a black vs. white, them vs. us confrontation. Bill, the Norfolk boy, who has the last word in *Coot Club* on the subject of the "Hullabaloos" ("They only got themselves to thank" [*CC*, 351]), oversimplifies the situation; simply because they are on the water, these ignorant, loud, crass, and vulgar people partake of the ethic of the waterside, willy-nilly. When they get their just deserts and are humiliated and very nearly drowned, Tom Dudgeon sees another side to the coin: "After all, even if while they had her they had used her to make things uncomfortable for other people, upsetting old ladies in their houseboats, throwing dinghies against quays and tearing down the banks with their wash, even if they had carried their horrible hullabaloo into the quietest corners of the Broads, they now were shipwrecked sailors" (*CC*, 344). Similarly, earlier, "into Tom's head came a picture of the *Margoletta* as a hostile owl, mobbed by a lot of small birds" (*CC*, 77).

But, on the whole, the Hullabaloos are seen as unredeemedly bad and stupid. They wear gaudy pajamas (in a place where sea boots are mandatory, another violation of the code); they make a continual awful noise; they have "loud, unreal laughter." Other cruisers, although noisy and polluting, may yet behave decently (*CC*, 105–6); the *Margoletta,* by contrast, rocks the crockery off the houseboat shelves of "little Miss Millett" (*CC*, 50), and her crew laughs at nearly swamping Mrs. Barrable (*CC*, 92). Mrs. Barrable, however, because she is really "Norfolk," is more than a match for them, in her quiet way. When they retreat in the face of her mild suggestion to the local po-

HULLABALOOS!

liceman that they could be prosecuted (as, indeed, a modern trans-
gressor certainly would be), we see again a conspiracy of superiority
against outsiders. "'I wouldn't do nothin' about it, ma'am,' said Mr.
Tedder [the policeman] slowly. 'They hear what you say. . . . Takes all
sorts to make a world, but fare to me as we could do without some of
'em'" (*CC*, 97).

Mrs. Barrable is the Captain Flint of the Broads books—a fallible
character, by turns romantic and practical and rash. She loads the
dice against the villains in a rather dangerous manner for an author
("What can your George Owdon (horrid name) have told them . . . ?"
[*CC*, 150]), admires Tom's morals ("That's a very good boy" [*CC*, 73]),
and puts Tom's mother in her place ("You run away, my dear" [*CC*,
88]). Her very ambiguity gives her rather more character than the
rest of the "new" cast.

Tom, a stalwart and pragmatic boy, who has a less rigorous relationship with his father than John Walker has with his (Dr. Dudgeon
is not interested in boats), is another of Ransome's "decent" heroes.
His family background—with a doctor father, a new baby, and his
father's patients (known as "victims") a constant feature of his
house—is sketched through incidental details. His friends, the twins
Port and Starboard, are less distinguishable, but their loyalty to their
widowed father gives a depth that might otherwise be lacking. Perhaps the most attractive characters, who demonstrate Ransome's
easy ability to move between classes, are the "Death and Glories,"
the three small boys who become the central characters of *The Big
Six*. In *Coot Club* they speak a rather broader dialect than in the
second book ("But how didn't they cotch ye?" [*CC*, 84]), which would,
perhaps, have been difficult to sustain. Similarly, only the early
drafts of *The River Comes First* were in dialect [*CN*, 25].

And so when, in *Coot Club*, Ransome's child characters set out on
their voyages around the Broads, they are surrounded by a three-
dimensional world, not only of real places but of shrewdly observed
characters. The very shape of the Broads—slowly flowing, winding
rivers—seems to *involve* people more than the static, wide reaches of
the Lake District in the north. The Lake District characters, as we
have seen, come gradually to populate the landscape. By the end of
a single book about the Norfolk Broads, we have been introduced to
a wide spectrum of waterborne and waterside life as the rivers and
the characters flow by—from the old eelman, who plays a larger part
in *The Big Six* (*CC*, 200), to Old Simon in the wherry, who admon-
ishes Port and Starboard for overcooking the bacon (*CC*, 235).

As we have seen, the voyage is on real waters, and Ransome occasionally betrays this actuality by his use of the present tense. When
Tom takes *Teasle* through Acle Bridge, he has to run her into the

bank: "*Teasle* hit the bank a little harder than Tom intended, but the bank is soft mud, and a great many people hit it harder still" (*CC*, 211–12). Likewise there is reference to the church at Beccles, "which is built, so to speak, in two bits, the tower in one bit and the rest of the church in another" (*CC*, 271).

Ransome's incidental descriptions are more lyrical than in any other book apart from *Swallowdale*, and reflect the different perspectives of the landscape. For instance, there is the long, idyllic sail, "While the Wind Holds," (chapter 20) onto the southern rivers in the twilight, and a pastoral as Tom Dudgeon paddles home: "The sun had gone down. The tide was on the point of turning, and up-river a calm green-and-golden glow filled the sky and was reflected in the scarcely moving water. A heron came flying downstream with long slow flaps of his great wings. Only twenty yards away he lifted easily over the tall reeds and settled with a noisy disturbance of twigs on the top of a tree in a little wood at the edge of the marshes" (*CC*, 75–76). At many points Ransome gives small, well-observed details, such as the marsh harriers tossing food to each other in flight (*CC*, 165–66).

But the basic concept of the cruise is not merely to introduce a beloved landscape or to give a setting for what is, after all, a rudimentary plot. Rather, it allows all the characters (and thus the reader) to see things afresh: "With everything being new to the apprentices, Tom and the twins, who knew the river by heart, felt almost as if they, too, were seeing it for the first time" (*CC*, 155).

This new perspective applies to Dorothea in a slightly different way. Her tendency to daydream into her unending novels (*CC*, 115) produces a gentle comment on the difference between fiction and reality, reminiscent of Ransome's equally gentle insights into the psychology of Bridget in *Swallows and Amazons*. She has been imagining meeting Port and Starboard: "Dorothea was finding, all of a sudden, that now that these sailing twins were close at hand, she did not know what to say to them. She found it easy enough to make up stories in which everyone talked and talked. Indeed, already, since yesterday, she had gone through half a dozen imaginary scenes in which she and Dick met and made friends with Port and Starboard. And now here they were, and she could not get one single word out of her mouth and was quite glad that William was doing all the talking and doing it very loud" (*CC*, 100). Somewhat later, "Dorothea, alone in the well, laid a daring hand on the tiller. This, indeed, was life" (*CC*, 104).

Whereas *Pigeon Post* opens with many crossreferences to the other books, here such reference actually works against cozy familiarity. Although Dick and Dorothea are accepted tolerantly, as we will see with the Swallows in *Secret Water*, other people's games are unimportant. When Dorothea, on hearing about Tom's casting off of the *Margoletta*, says, "It's just what Nancy would have done. Nancy's a girl we know," Tom Dudgeon reflects that "whoever Nancy was, that made no difference to Tom who . . . had done the one forbidden thing" (*CC*, 70–71). Similarly, when they are on Oulton Broad and are overtaken by a squall (known, Ransome says, in Norfolk, as a "Roger"), Dorothea laughs, "'Give him some chocolate. The Roger we know's always ready for some.' But the Coots hardly heard her. Things were much too serious" (*CC*, 279).

All of this is in the context of real sailing. Whereas Dick and Dorothea can be taught the names of ropes and be dazzled by the paraphernalia of sailing, the more knowledgeable children can be mesmerized by the deckhand of the Thames barge, with the delicious litany of knots: "And then he settled down on a hatch and showed them all kinds of knots and other things that can be made with rope, Bowlines and Fisherman's and Carrick bends, Rolling, Blackwall, Timber and Handspike hitches, Cat's Paws and Sheepshanks, Eye splices and Long splices, Grommets and a Selvagee strop" (*CC*, 274).

Structurally, at first, the book seems to be broken-backed, with two distinct parts, the first somewhat dense and domestic, the other a matter of distances and journeys. The motivation seems a little crude, the ending a trifle contrived, with almost all the characters crowding onstage. However, the two parts of the book are also marked by the distinction between tidal and nontidal waters. In the first part, the waters are predictable; in the second, they require a different level of skill—they are more dangerous and more challenging. Tom's only sailing mistake is caused by the tide (when he bumps *Teasle* on Reedham Bridge), and the Hullabaloos' disaster is similarly caused. On this symbolic level, the book has much more coherence.

But most strikingly in *Coot Club*, as in *Swallowdale*, Ransome is not afraid of the rainy day. The book has dull days as well as days of excitement, and Ransome skillfully changes pace between chapters. As Fielding, a robust eighteenth-century writer whom Ransome must have admired, says in *Tom Jones*, "My reader, then, is not to be surprised if in the course of this work he shall find some chapters very short, and others altogether as long; some that contain only the time of a single day, and others that comprise years; in a word, if my history sometimes seems to stand still and sometimes to fly."[4]

Thus the first day takes six chapters, the second, three; chapter 10 covers three days, whereas day 6 takes three chapters and day 7, two. On the southern waters, in part 2, day 8 and day 9 take four chapters each; chapter 23 covers one day and chapter 24, two days; whereas the last day needs five chapters to itself. Each burst of activity needs a recuperating period; balance and reassurance are vital to Ransome.

Coot Club also contains one un-Ransome-like, and to some readers immortal, character: William the pug-dog. This is about the only occasion in the whole canon where Ransome indulges his sense of whimsy; William is drawn both from the inside and the outside—in fact, given a page of pure pug-thoughts. "William . . . had had a rather upsetting day. . . . He had lain as usual on the foredeck . . . knowing that he made a noble sight for anyone who might be sailing up and down the river. He went back to the well and heard Dorothea say what a handsome pug he was. . . . He was annoyed to find some of [Mrs. Barrable's] paint-brushes soaking in a jam-pot half full of turpentine. . . . If he had not been prudent in sniffing, that turpentine could have ruined his nose for a week" (*CC,* 60). So when William "put into his barking all he thought about boys who startled honest pugs by lying hid in reeds so that the honest pugs ran into them face to face on their own level" (*CC,* 66), or when he is weighed ("Hardworking and Successful" [*CC,* 159]) or dumped into the mud ("And after all this talk about wiping paws on the mat" [*CC,* 323]), we see a very amiable anthropomorphism. Possibly the personality of the real-life William (who belonged to Ransome's friends, the Renolds) overwhelmed Ransome.[5] He can also take a less whimsical view, as when William comes out of the cabin when the *Teasle* jibes on their way downriver, "as if to warn people that things like that must not happen again" (*CC,* 199).

The Coots are a practical, unromantic bunch who tolerate the incomers, but by the end of the book, Dick and Dorothea have at least partial acceptance into their world. They are viewed with much more sympathy than they were in *Winter Holiday*—perhaps because the codes of the Coot Club are a good deal more practical and less literary–romantic than those of the Swallows and Amazons, and partly because the Coot Club encompasses children of all classes. For example, when Dick, learning to quant, falls into the water, "He was astonished to find that everybody was very pleased with him" (*CC,* 168). It is an initiation.

Thus the nonsailing child reader can identify with the D.'s rather more directly than with the Swallows; they are closer to unexceptional reality. This may be why, as the whole series progresses, the D.'s grow in stature at the expense of the Amazons (it is Dick who has the last word of all, in *Great Northern?*). Ransome quietly stresses their mutual loyalty ("Dorothea did not feel that the twins half understood how useful [Dick] could be" [*CC,* 320]) and regards them affectionately, as when they compare hands: "They're so beautifully horny" (*CC,* 183). By the end of the book, they are well on their way toward the full acceptance that comes in the autumn.

The Big Six

"Pete had a loose tooth, and could not keep his tongue from jiggling it" (*BS*, 17). So begins *Coot Club*'s more distinguished successor, bringing to the fore Ransome's working-class characters, Joe, Bill, and Pete of the *Death and Glory,* and imparting a very different flavor to the text.

The Big Six (1940) is a plot-based novel, with a dual emphasis on the contrast between the middle classes and the working classes, and the necessity of collecting concrete evidence to clear the Death and Glories' names. Fishing and sailing, as ever, provide the freemasonry that links the two strands with the people and landscape.

As in *Coot Club,* the "middle-class" parents react sympathetically to the children's difficulties, but with a judicious consideration of the evidence, whereas the parents of Joe, Bill, and Pete are more direct. For example, when the boys are first accused, Pete's father is among the crowd at the Staithe.

> Pete's father listened.
> "Shurrup," he said suddenly. "Pete. You tell me. Have you touch any of them boats?"
> "No," said Pete.
> "Hear that," said Pete's father. (*BS*, 69–71)

Later on, the father gets into a fight over the accusation. Many conventional children's books thrive on the opposition of stupid adults and clever children; in *The Big Six,* when Mr. Tedder is unsympathetic (as the plot requires him to be), the working-class parents react against him. At no point is the real world pushed away or any special favors done to the children. As Joe's mother says, "Casting off boats and that is no good in a place like this, and Hannam's would have sacked your Dad if he weren't too good a boatbuilder to lose" (*BS*, 273). This authenticity elevates *The Big Six* from the conventional to the convincing. For example, it provides more than a suggestion that the boys are being persecuted because they are at the bottom of the social heap; as a result, they do not find Dorothea's cheerful fictionalizing of events particularly funny.

> "What's the camera for?" asked Bill.
> "Photographing clues," said Dick.
> "When there's a murder," said Dorothea, "they always dash in and photograph everything."
> "But there ain't a murder, not yet," said Bill.

"There may be," said Dorothea excitedly. "The villain
fights like a rat once he's cornered."
Bill, despairing of Dorothea, turned to Tom. "We ain't none
of us villains," he said. "You know that." (*BS*, 186–87)

The character most sympathetic towards the boys is the fisherman, intending to spend the winter on his specially designed boat.
Not only does this Ransome-like figure appear in key fishing scenes,
but he advances the plot; when he pays the boys the large sum of
thirty shillings (about three dollars) for catching a record fish, he
swears them to secrecy. (The payment also provides the opportunity
for a food orgy—"steak and kidney, stewed oxtail, corned beef, peas,
beans, pears, peaches, marmalade and strawberry jam" [*BS*, 130].)
Similarly, fishing gives Ransome the opportunity for brief but
closely observed pieces of scene setting, in his most mature manner:
"The morning mist was heavy on the river and on the sodden fields
that lay on either side of it. The fields were below the level of the
river and the Death and Glories, marching along the rond that kept
the river from overflowing, looked down on feeding cattle and horses
whose thick coats were pale with moisture. Joe walking in front along
the narrow path startled a great carthorse which went suddenly
thundering away, its shaggy hoofs splashing as they struck the wet
ground" (*BS*, 98).
Moreover, as in his fishing books, this rural idyll is closely linked
to the exciting business of catching fish. The fisherman goes to get
milk from the local inn, leaving the boys in charge of his pike-fishing
tackle. The bait is taken by a huge pike, and Joe plays him, while the
others blow the foghorn and shout for help. The pike makes a dash
into the reeds: "Joe pulled. It was as if he were pulling at a haystack.
He wound at the reel till the rod tip was in the water. He tried to lift.
The line rose, quivering and dripping. Joe let the reel spin to ease it.
It was no good. Deep in the reeds the pike lay still" (*BS*, 107). Pete,
like a spaniel, stamps into the river after it, and the battle recomm-
ences. When the fisherman returns, he takes the boys very seriously;
they have a laconic exchange, as between peers:

"You take him," said Joe, looking over his shoulder.
"How long have you had him on?" asked the fisherman.
"Year or two," said Joe shortly.
"Carry on for another month, then. . . . You've hooked him,
You've held him. You've played him. I'm not going to take
the rod now." (*BS*, 109)

The fisherman, having won his bet on the size of the fish from the landlord of the Roaring Donkey Inn, gives the boys the money, and here it is quite clear that the boys do not live in a privileged world. On their way back to Horning they reflect on what the landlord would say if he knew: "None too pleased he won't be," said Joe. "Why, if he'd have known we caught it, he'd have given us half a crown [about twenty cents] and we'd have thought we done well. But thirty bob [shillings] and a tanner [a six-penny piece] . . . There's many a man don't earn that in a week" (*BS*, 126–27).

This solidity of detail and realism of attitude place *The Big Six* in the same category as *We Didn't Mean to Go to Sea* and *The Picts and the Martyrs*. Ransome himself called the pike scene "a very gorgeous episode," and like smoking the eels or lighting the Christmas pudding with methylated spirits, this scene existed before the rest of the book.[6]

All such apparent digressions are integral to the plot itself. When the boys visit the old eelman, Ransome is able to indulge in some meticulous reportage, but the episode also provides an alibi. Ransome clearly identifies closely with the area. The houseboat in which "the eelman lived and mended his nets and watched the river" is described with Ransome's anthropological eye. A sense of timelessness pervades the eelman's cabin and his lifestyle. Both are reminiscent of Captain Konga and the hulk of the *Toledo* in the Baltic in *Racundra's First Cruise* (*RFC*, 120–21):

There was a bunk along one side, with a patchwork bedspread over it. There was a table under one of the windows. There was a bench beside it. An old Jack Tar stove was in the middle of the floor, nearly red hot, with a big black kettle singing on the top of it. A long-barrelled, ancient gun hung from a couple of nails on the wall over the bunk. There were shelves with all kinds of gear, weights for nets, coiled eel-lines with their twenty or thirty hooks stuck in a cork that rested in the middle of the coil. On the table was a big pair of steel-rimmed spectacles, with all the metal work painted white to keep off the rust. The walls were covered with pictures cut out of newspapers, brown and smoky with age, pictures of Queen Victoria's Jubilee, pictures of soldiers off to South Africa [1899], and pictures of the Coronation of Edward the Seventh [1902]. The old man's interest in history seemed to have stopped about then, for there were no pictures of anything that happened later. (*BS*, 49–50)

The basic Ransome codes are reinforced. The boys are hurt because the crimes have been "patched" onto them; not merely because they did not do them, but because they are accused of violating the very things of which they are most professionally proud. When Tom's father questions whether just one of the three might be doing it, Tom protests: "They wouldn't . . . Not one of them. Boats matter more than anything else to them. More than birds. Not one of them would do it" (*BS*, 306–7).

Similarly, Ransome's unspoken ethic is always for truth. Tom's mother can tell that they are telling the truth, as can the friendly fisherman, who is, of course, of the elect and perhaps influenced by the fact that one of the Coot Club rules is always to bury orange peel: "'Well,' said the fisherman, 'it's a pretty good rule, and it'll take a lot to make me believe that you chaps cast off other people's boats.'" (*BS*, 327). As Bill says, after watching the villains casting off the *Cachalot*, "You see, if they asks me I can't say I weren't there" (*BS*, 365).

Not everyone agrees with this positive assessment of the characters. When *The Big Six* was published, Rosamond Lehmann, writing in the *New Statesman*, produced a very sardonic review, commenting on Ransome's "almost grinding insistence on matters of technical proficiency." She then dealt with the characters. "As usual, the characters are flat, colourless, humourless, totally external; symbols of cooperative efficiency. I don't know why I always rather dislike them: I suppose it is because they are always so on the spot, up to the mark, and, somehow, sterilised."[7]

Ironically, and perhaps with somewhat dubious professional ethics, her final comment, "Every boy will vote this detective story super," has been quoted as approbation on the dust-jackets of the books for at least thirty years—*without* its deprecatory qualification ("But that is beside the point").

Ransome is too honest a writer to allow the virtue of his characters to go unchallenged. The idea of bird-protection and conservation, so fashionable today, had its critics even in 1940 (or 1933). Talking to the eelman Harry Bangate, the Coot Club members have something of a shock. The old man is reminiscing about his youth: "There weren't no houses at Potter [Heigham, a village] then, saving the wind-pumps. And there weren't no yachts, hardly. Reed-boats and such, and the wherries loading by the bridge. And there were plenty of netting then, and liggering for pike, and plenty of fowl. . . . In old days we shoot a plenty and there were plenty for all to shoot." Tom objects that this is why the birds disappeared. The old man is not convinced:

"Don't you believe it. . . . They go what with the reed cutting and all they pleasure boats. . . ."

Tom looked at the faces of the other Coots, to see how they were taking these awful heresies. . . . It was no good arguing with old Harry, but, after all, it was one thing for an old Broadsman to talk about taking bitterns' eggs and quite another for somebody like George Owdon who had plenty of pocket money already without robbing birds.

The old man caught the look on Pete's face.

"Old thief. Old Harry Bangate," he said. "That's what you think. And I say, No. What was them birds put there for? Why, for shooting." (*BS*, 52–53)

All of this is quite close to Jefferies in *Bevis* and *The Gamekeeper at Home;* the ambiguity of the true countryman, who can simultaneously love and kill, is shown very clearly.

Ransome's skill in dovetailing events is particularly suited to the detective mode, while "the exploration of the avenues," as Dorothea puts it (*BS*, 228), also allows him to create a landscape that exists at many points simultaneously rather than one, as in *Coot Club,* that is linear with the flow of the rivers.

The contrast between the romantic and the practical is continued into characterization. Dick and Tom are rather more mechanical figures; Dorothea provides the contrast: "'I'm being the villain,' said Dorothea. . . . 'Bet he ain't got no plait to pull,' said Joe, but was instantly ashamed of himself when he saw the serious way Dick was looking at his sister" (*BS*, 310). Despite, or perhaps because of, the conventions of the genre in which Ransome is working, the de-romanticizing of fiction is also continued. Dorothea is speculating about what would happen if the villain were to catch Tom: "'The river's so handy. A splash . . . A groan . . . Just a few bubbles in the dark. . . .' 'There'd be more'n a few bubbles if anybody push Tom Dudgeon in the river. Take a tidy villain to push him in,' said Pete" (*BS*, 339).

Most of all, *The Big Six,* written in the desperate days at the beginning of World War II, is an optimistic book. Evil can be defeated, even (and especially) by the weakest. The two children least qualified in the skilled world of sailors, Dick and Pete, supply the key piece of evidence; the sole girl in the cast masterminds the operation; the combined efforts of all the classes win through. Ransome was advised by his publishers to "steer clear of the war at all costs."[8] He did so, literally, but it is possible to read *The Big Six* (and possibly *The Picts and the Martyrs*) as unconscious commentaries on the struggle.

The envoi, where we leave the Death and Glories almost for the last time, is, appropriately, a fishing joke that looks forward to a bright future. As they stand in the Roaring Donkey Inn, looking at the newly stuffed and mounted monster pike, an old fisherman turns to them:

> "Are you the boys who caught that fish?". . .
>   "We didn't exactly . . ." began Joe.
>   "Poor lads," said the old man. "Poor lads. . . . So young and with nothing left to live for."
>   "Let's go and catch another," said Pete. (*BS,* 399)

7

Deep and Shallow Waters: *We Didn't Mean to Go to Sea* and *Secret Water*

On 15 January 1936, Ransome wrote to Wren Howard, of Jonathan Cape: "During the last four days I have seen, grabbed, clutched and pinioned a really gorgeous idea for another book. . . . Lovely new angle of technical approach. . . . There are EIGHT words in its entirely admirable memorable and inevitable title."[1] (Presumably, Ransome originally thought of it as *We Did Not Mean to Go to Sea*.) Ransome's enthusiasm was justified, for it is generally agreed by critics that in *We Didn't Mean to Go to Sea* he wrote his masterpiece. One of the first reviewers, Amabel Williams-Ellis in the *Manchester Guardian*, commented upon the "inevitability of the plot. . . . At every turn readers will agree 'so and not otherwise.'"[2]

If, as Kit Pearson suggests, many of the "Swallows and Amazons" series can be seen as parts of a single book,[3] then *We Didn't Mean to Go to Sea* and *Secret Water* can be seen as a single unit within that magnum opus.

Sequentially, they follow the rather wild adventure of *Pigeon Post*, but Ransome has shifted not only the place—initially at least, to the River Orwell in Sussex—but the focus. The Walker family are alone in *We Didn't Mean to Go to Sea*, and center stage in *Secret Water*. These changes lead to his most mature character writing as well as his most distinguished narrative, both structurally and in specific action sequences. The characters now act, rather than reacting within a large group; their individuality, which previously tended to be signalled or labelled, now has the room actually to develop. Their identity as a family is taken for granted; we can now watch the dynamics of their relationships. The Walkers grow up so much in *We*

Didn't Mean to Go to Sea that Ransome does not use them again in a "realistic" book (apart from *Secret Water*); he only uses their names in *Missee Lee* and *Great Northern?*.

We Didn't Mean to Go to Sea

Fred Inglis, who has a very high opinion of this book, notes that "Ransome was not a reflective writer, nor even one, it seems, who busied himself with the expression of emotion at all (he resists the notion that literature is there for the expression of personal feeling). The circumstances of *We Didn't Mean to Go to Sea* [1937] allow personal feeling to transpire straight from action and not reflection. Events from outside force right conduct on those with the knowledge to perform it. Right conduct brings right feeling."[4]

Structurally, *We Didn't Mean to Go to Sea* is among the most interesting of the sequence, although by far the simplest. Indeed, this simplicity worried Ransome. In March 1937 he wrote to a friend, "The trouble is that one single incident fills the book, that reality presses so hard on the children that there is no room or need for romantic transfiguration of fact."[5]

We have already seen the way in which Ransome manipulates the themes of family and displacement and the way in which, in the Lake District novels, he has gradually extended the symbolic maturity of his characters. *We Didn't Mean to Go to Sea*, with its "real" dangers, takes the relationship between story and story shape to its logical conclusion. After it, *Secret Water* acts as a coda, restoring us to a fictive world.

As Inglis observes, "Ransome's touch and pacing are faultless. We are a third of the way through the book before the awful moment at which they realize the *Goblin* is dragging her anchor. . . . The tranquility and pleasure of the first part of the novel are sharpened by the tension with which we wait for the adventure."[6]

Thus the first 107 pages in the original edition constitute the buildup to the main action: as in a fairy tale, the children are given the skills necessary to survive and the rules they have to obey. In the second part, because of their lack of experience, they drift out to sea, but then they take control of their fate and sail across the North Sea. Toward the end of this episode they are sufficiently in control of the ship to rescue the kitten. The remaining seventy-six pages form a coda; Daddy is in control; the great, unseen controlling force is finally personified. Ransome comes close to overwriting the scene: "And Titty, watching him, found herself smiling in the funny quiet way Mother sometimes smiled when she talked of the things Daddy had done long ago. Daddy was certainly very unlike anybody else. Captain Flint could be counted on in the same sort of way, but even Captain Flint . . . would have been in a hurry to know all about it, how it had all happened, and so on. But Daddy . . . was asking no questions at all" (*WDM*, 279). (Hugh Brogan feels that this is not so much a literary matter as a biographical one: "In *We Didn't Mean to Go to Sea*, [Arthur] at last settled accounts with Cyril Ransome . . . for his daydream of at last earning and winning the approval that had been so rigidly withheld had at length given him the theme for a book of which Conrad would have been proud.")[7] This, then, is the father whose permission was central to the first book, and whose presence sits over the whole of *We Didn't Mean to Go to Sea*.

Geoffrey Trease, in his pioneering survey *Tales Out of School,* first published in 1949, observes that in children's books, "Parenthood is practically a capital offence," and he quotes Dorothy Neal White's *About Books for Children*: "The basic relationship which children know is the parent-child relationship, yet in the majority of tales authors do not even try to handle this theme; they exile father to Poona."[8] As we have seen, although Ransome seems to adopt this device, in fact the parents are always present in spirit. *We Didn't Mean to Go to Sea* is the extreme case of the children's living up to the invisible parental ideal, and it is fitting that the parent should then appear in the flesh.

The "frame" of the book is extremely strong. Some readers may cavil about the extraordinary coincidence that is the key to the book, but it is needed to counterbalance the very real danger that the children have been in. Conversely, the episode with the pilot, an unintentionally threatening introduction to a friendly country, counterbalances the momentary feeling of confidence that rescuing the kitten has given them. Margery Fisher comments that the "transfiguration of fact" is present in *We Didn't Mean to Go to Sea*, "but in a different way."[9] That transfiguration is structural.

The structure is closely integrated with the portrayal of the family; everything depends on the interaction among the children *as parts of the family,* and as bounded by family codes and family circumstances. Thus, from the first sentence, the family hierarchy (a sexist one, of course) is established: "John was at the oars; Roger was in the bows; Susan and Titty were sitting side by side in the stern of a borrowed dinghy" (*WDM*, 17). The security, the very Englishness of the place, is established very firmly: "Only the evening before they had come down the deep green lane that ended in the river itself. . . . Last night they had slept for the first time at Alma Cottage, and this morning had waked for the first time to look out through Miss Powell's climbing roses at this happy place where almost everybody wore

AMONG THE MOORED YACHTS

sea-boots, and land, in comparison with water, seemed hardly to matter at all" (*WDM,* 17). The family is complete with Bridget, who has
been growing up as fast as she can (*WDM,* 37).

Mrs. Walker thinks things over overnight, and gets testimonials
for Jim Brading before allowing them to leave. (Mrs. Walker is, of
course, one of the elite: "I say, your mother knows how to handle a
boat" [*WDM,* 44].) Permission is equally granted from the ultimate
authority, Commander Walker: "Grab a chance and you won't be
sorry for a might-have-been" (*WDM,* 37). Indeed, "Daddy" is frequently quoted, from the second page (Daddy's opinions on square
sterns) onwards. Family codes of fairness and good behavior, as well
as solidarity, are equally stressed. When they telephone home from
Shotley, Susan speaks to Bridget:

> "What did Bridget want?" asked Titty.
> "Only to say that she was going to sleep in Mother's room,"
> said Susan.

They were silent as they left the inn and started back to the pier. It was funny how that single sentence made them feel almost like deserters. Bridget was sleeping in Mother's room because the expedition in the *Goblin* had left Alma Cottage a rather lonely place for both of them. (*WDM,* 74)

For the next hundred pages, the initiation of the children into the skills necessary to survival is also linked to their roles. They learn about buoys, lightships, and steamers' signals and are introduced to the idea of the human sharks who steal grounded boats, and the shame of the sailor who runs aground—or, indeed, takes a pilot. All of this is not only good sense ("Only one motto for the *Goblin.* When in doubt keep clear of shoals. . . . Get out to sea and stay there" [*WDM,* 71]) and plot motivation but also a matter of pride: John is being initiated into the brotherhood of adult sailing. As Margery Fisher notes, "He is young, though trying hard not to be, and because his sense of proportion is that of a boy of thirteen or so he takes literally Jim Brading's casual warnings."[10]

Retrospectively, the preparation is, as in Ransome's Russian folktales, very specific. John has a lesson on reefing, with the "little brass crank" that he later nearly loses overboard (*WDM,* 42, 168); Roger plays with the Woolworth unbreakable plates—"'Good as a port light,' Jim had said, and [he] had held the plate in front of the torch and had lit up everybody's face in turn with a warm red glow," a glow that later saves them from being run down by the steamer in the dark (*WDM,* 68, 180–81); and Roger practices his penny whistle, which, when they take a pilot, supplies the "grown-up noises below" (*WDM,* 75, 259–60). They find out about the bilge pump, what to do in fog, and how to signal for a pilot (Titty puts the flag away—"We shan't want a pilot flag on this voyage," she says regretfully—but of course she gets it out again at Flushing [*WDM,* 87, 252]).

Jim's advice is sometimes melodramatic ("So, if you're ever in trouble, never take a tow from anybody if you can help it, and never ever let anyone come aboard. Bang their hands with a boathook. Do anything you like, but keep them off. . . . The only people to take aboard are pilots, and you don't want even to take a pilot if you can help it [*WDM,* 70]); but, after all, he is very young himself, and Ransome pokes gentle fun as he learns to smoke a pipe ("The others were watching him with respect" [*WDM,* 41]).

The device of distancing and contrast is used throughout, both to provide a pause and some dramatic irony and to reinforce family ties. When they first move off downriver, we momentarily remain behind on the "hard" with Bridget, Mrs. Walker, and Miss Powell. "'Don't you wish you were going too?' said Miss Powell to Bridget. 'Somebody had to stay and look after Mother,' said Bridget. . . . Far away down the river the little red-sailed *Goblin,* with the small black *Imp* dancing astern of her, disappeared behind a moored steamer" (*WDM,* 52).

Even more effective is the interruption of the voyage, after the encounter with the steamer (and the use of the Woolworth plate), by a narrative visit to Pin Mill. Mother and Bridget, in the relatively peaceful bedroom in Alma Cottage, talk about the storm, and Bridget sees that "Mother in her white nightgown was out of bed and had gone to the window and was looking out into the night, listening to the wind" (*WDM,* 188). Since we know what is happening, this scene allows the child reader to feel both superior and sympathetic to Mrs. Walker.

As in *Coot Club,* there is a symbolic as well as actual change between inland waters and the sea. The catastrophe is enacted in the harbor, on the very edge of deep water, and involves the breaking of codes. Ransome's attitude to engines throughout the sequence is, at best, ambivalent (perhaps reminiscent of the intractable engine in *Racundra*), and here it is the engine that precipitates the catastrophe. (Only towards the end of the book does the engine rehabilitate itself in terms of the code: "But to-day, even John, who cared for nothing but sail, was grateful to the little engine chug-chugging away under the companion steps. It had saved them at the very last minute and was taking them quickly further and further away from the danger of a broken promise" (*WDM,* 91).) Jim has forgotten to refill the fuel tanks; he then breaks another rule by leaving the ship, and the atmosphere slowly changes: "Jim had been away so long that the pleasure of having the ship to themselves came to an end" (*WDM,* 100). This is where *We Didn't Mean to Go to Sea* really begins.

The slow tension, based on things *not* being done and said, carries the children out toward the sea. From this point we begin to see genuine interaction and a cutting away from the games of childhood. However well-prepared they are (although they may not know it), these are still four children, in the fog, about to drift onto a real sea.

They initially fall back on their accustomed roles: Roger retreats into doing as he is told, and survives on faith; Titty retreats into herself (and illness). John, as far as he can, follows his role models, Jim Brading and his father. In Susan, previously a stereotyped character, the clash of theory (and perhaps fiction) and reality is expressed most forcibly; hence she begins to grow, and her growth is linked to family structures and to the larger structures of the book. ("Roger pulled at Titty's elbow. 'Susan's going to cry,' he whispered. 'Look the other way,' said Titty" [*WDM,* 126].)

In some ways, Susan now becomes the voice of the nonexpert against the expert. What, after all, would a nonsailor do, faced with that situation? She argues for the simple and obvious solution and is not only proven wrong (when John turns the *Goblin* round), but virtually accused of betraying the code. Turning round is a brutal experience, prefaced by Ransome's calm, sailorlike assessment: "You never know quite how hard the wind is blowing when you are sailing with it. It is a very different thing when you come to turn against it" (*WDM*, 156). Susan pays the price of her treason, while Roger sits in the bottom of the cockpit and John hangs on: "And Susan, shaken almost to pieces with this new violent motion of the battling ship, lay half across the cockpit, with her head over the coaming, and was sick. A wave broke across the cabin roof and a lump of green water hit her on the side of the head" (*WDM*, 157). The Susan that emerges from this experience is not one that will easily play games again on the lake: "She lifted her head. [John] saw something that was hardly Susan's face, blotched and white, with wisps of bedraggled hair across her eyes, a face wet with rain and tears" (*WDM*, 163). Being seasick is not like the ironic affair of *Peter Duck*. Titty goes below. Susan goes down to help her, but is forced to come up, and "she was sick over the side. She was sick again and again. When it was over she remembered she was in the way so that John could not see the compass. . . . 'Susan,' said John at last. 'Poor old chap'" (*WDM*, 146).

John's turn of phrase may well be seen as more than a colloquialism (equal, perhaps, to the unisex "guys" of today). Ransome is undeniably sexist; girls simply do not survive as well as boys, and even Roger isn't seasick ("'Don't you feel seasick at all?' said Susan almost angrily. 'Not a bit'" [*WDM*, 159]). As in the climactic reefing scene, Susan suffers dramatically from the necessity that she be less quick on the uptake than the reader. Otherwise, as Fisher notes, "In Susan we see a girl who is well aware of the difference between the adult world and the world of children."[11]

The empathy between Titty, the romantic, and John, who is rapidly growing into a true sailor, transcends the rather obvious male/female stereotypes. What is important is the romance of the sea, and Titty and John both feel it: "John was enjoying the thought that they had the ship to themselves. . . . He told himself secretly that he had just sailed the *Goblin* from Dover and was waiting to take the tide up the river. 'John,' said Titty. 'Where've we come from?' John started. It was as if she had heard him speak his thought aloud. 'River Plate,' he said. Dover seemed too near, if Titty was also thinking they had come in from the sea" (*WDM*, 94).

In many ways, John Walker, although essentially serious and humorless, does prove the virtues of the code. He learns the meaning of danger ("Lonely? It was as if he were outside life altogether and wouldn't be alive again till he got back" [*WDM*, 166]) but holds on to fatherly advice ("'One hand for yourself and one for the ship.' His father had told him years ago. . . . What was it Daddy had said? 'Never be ashamed to reef in the dark'" [*WDM,* 167, 170]). Most profoundly, John understands the mystique of sailing: "He, for that night, was the Master of the *Goblin,* and even the lurches of the cockpit beneath him as the *Goblin* rushed through the dark filled him with a serious kind of joy" (*WDM,* 200).

Only John's hubristic escape from death and his triumph over the technicalities of the *Goblin* make (as Titty perceives it) "the ship . . . suddenly full of happiness" (*WDM,* 172). The cabin lamp is symbolically lit; together they cope with the steamer. Susan recovers her poise (and her frame of reference; John has scraped his wrist; Susan looks for the iodine: "I'm sure mother'd say you ought to put some on" [*WDM,* 184]) and from there on the children begin to think positively of where they are going to, not where they have been: "The thing had been decided. From that moment on not one of them looked astern, not even Susan" (*WDM,* 219). They are growing up.

To emphasize this change, they rescue the kitten, an even weaker character than themselves, and they encounter another steamer and outface it: "John clenched his teeth. . . . 'Steam gives way to sail. . . . We've just got to keep straight on'. . . . And then, ever so slightly, the huge steamer did indeed give way to sail, but not an inch more than she had to" (*WDM,* 243).

When they come in sight of land and signal for a pilot, they become, as it were, children again—although children pretending to be adults and, in John's case, a boy-captain pretending to be a boy: "John tried his best to feel that he was not in charge of the ship but was only a ship's boy with nothing to worry about except his steering" (*WDM,* 257).

And so we are quite prepared for the reduction to child size when Commander Walker arrives. This is Ransome's most sentimental moment: "Susan . . . looking at Daddy, with his weather-beaten, brown face, and the wrinkles round his eyes, some from laughter, some from looking into wind and sun at sea . . . knew that whatever had happened everything was all right now" (*WDM,* 276). As Brogan comments, "for one dreadful moment it seems that something is going wrong with the book."[12] Powerful situations no doubt generate powerful feelings, but this particular display does verge on the embarrassing, for all its virtues as a strong closure: "But though he had never said so, they all knew that for some reason or other, Daddy was rather pleased with them than otherwise. There was something in the way he looked at John" (*WDM,* 288). That passage at least is preferable to the Kiplingesque "You'll be a seaman yet, my son" (*WDM,* 292).

The anonymous critic in the *Times Literary Supplement* wrote in

1950, "In the construction of his stories, he adopts the oldest and most successful of formulae, that of the classical tragedy, with the climax coming in Act Four"[13] In *We Didn't Mean to Go to Sea*, Ransome is again testing the limits of narrative formulae. Once the adventure is over, what can sustain the narrative? The answer must be a mature interest in human reactions. The coda is not merely a ballast to the adventure, it is a move toward a more mature kind of writing and reading.

Thus, *We Didn't Mean to Go to Sea* is a book founded solidly on reality; even when the children refer to fiction, it is to relate fiction to reality. When Roger asks Titty how many hoots on the foghorn to give, "Titty answered. Her head was throbbing and she was afraid she was going to be sick, but she did know something about fog signals. 'Three hoots,' she said, 'Sailing vessel with the wind aft. Remember *Peter Duck*'" (*WDM*, 137).[14] *Peter Duck* is italicized: she is referring to a *story*, not to the personal invention of *Swallowdale*. Once again, the virtue of the positive use of the book's place in a series is underlined; by a kind of shorthand, Titty can recall her former self and a complex network of reference.

As usual, the action is surrounded by carefully built up local detail. Ransome notes the "grave salute of East Coast Sailors," the porpoises, the seaplane base, "a Norwegian timber-ship with a tremendous deck-cargo of golden sawn planks" (*WDM*, 62), the ferry, and so on. The calm domestic life of early-morning swims, boiled eggs, and sleeping afloat are all lulls before the storm.

His images of sailing are, perhaps more than ever before, striking in their economy and appositeness. When the rain comes, "the ropes darkened and stiffened. . . . One rain-squall . . . would pass, and for a few minutes the seas seemed to widen out around them" (*WDM*, 152, 153).

To read *We Didn't Mean to Go to Sea* is to read a book that is a yardstick for children's literature. Not only does it epitomize Ransome's outlook and his valuing of skills and ethics of a certain kind, it establishes a relationship between the adult world and the child world that requires an increasingly mature response from the reader.

Secret Water

After the storms of *We Didn't Mean to Go to Sea, Secret Water* (1939), its immediate sequel, is a safe, domestic book. It may be no coincidence that it went through four British printings in its first month—November 1939, shortly after war was declared. It is also very much a "series" book, in a slightly negative sense; it would, one suspects, be scarcely comprehensible without some knowledge of the other books and of the relationship between the Walkers and the Blacketts.

Hardyment feels that it is "an elusive story" and that "it seems to be working on several different levels."[15] Certainly the Walker family is an awkward one, now, to be populating a children's book, partly because of their greater maturity and partly because of the way that experience has welded them into an exclusive, inward-looking society. The underlying conflict with the Blacketts, which we have seen throughout the series, now becomes, symbolically, open war. The Walkers have been given a task, to finish the map, again under the shadow of their father; Nancy and Peggy, without these familial obligations, wish to play games. Ransome's skill in building tension is undiminished, but it is tension of a different order: The question is, will they be ready on time? rather than, will they survive?

Brogan feels that the opening pages of *Secret Water* "are some of the most stiffly awkward that Ransome ever wrote.[16] Not everyone agrees. Wallace Hildick cites the porridge-eating scene in the second chapter (*SW*, 27) as an example of skillful pacing, "interrupting, or braking, the larger drama with one of the miniature dramas of childhood." Although Ransome takes a "considerable" risk, he succeeds through "great technical skill."[17]

From the outset, John and Titty, the most family-code-oriented of the Walkers, are anxious about the reaction of the Amazons. Nancy knows better than they how to cope with the shyness of the "mastodon" in the face of the newcomers ("'Greeting,' said Nancy, in the grand manner" [*SW*, 130]), but she has no idea how her friends have changed. Now responsibility to the task and to their father is paramount. The Amazons watch closely as the map is explained to them. Nancy comments that the area would be a grand place for a war.

> "But there won't be time for any war," said John. . . .
> For some time the Amazons watched in silence.
> "You'll get a medal from the Royal Geographical Society," said Nancy at last. . . . "The Walker Expedition."
> Both John and Titty noticed that she said "you" instead of "we." (*SW*, 136)

At this point, the friendship is ruptured.

Nevertheless, the byplay between the children is very much of those with shared experiences, who know each other's foibles, and who do work together happily, even though Nancy is reluctantly playing someone else's game and John, especially, does not join in with Nancy's games and jolly exclamations. Indeed, Nancy's comments sometimes border on the blasphemous: "If only it was always like

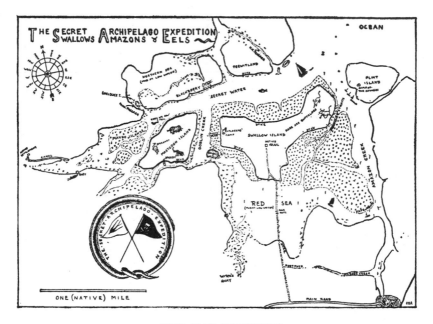

THE MAP COMPLETE

this. . . . So that we could sail anywhere, any time. I don't see the good of tides. What's the good of a sea if it's all going to be mud in a few hours." Titty corrects her: "It's like breathing. . . . When the tide's out, everything goes dead" (*SW*, 162). This is the difference between the inland sailors and the sea-sailors.

Equally, in the context of *We Didn't Mean to Go to Sea, Secret Water* is probably the most mechanical of the books. Everything, from the outset, is carefully controlled; no plot thrust holds the themes together, and, like *Winter Holiday,* it is all a little easy. As Fisher points out, the characters have such "technical expertise" that "in the way the Walkers reach out to conquer a new territory there is even an imperialist touch"[18] This may be why the creation of another set of children, the Mastodon, Daisy, Dum, and Dee (rather reminiscent of *Coot Club*) is relatively unsuccessful. Although they are potentially characters in their own right, they have little to do. No room is left for much characterization.

Ransome based the "Eels" on children of a friend of his, Colonel Busk, but only the skinny Daisy takes on a real, prickly life. Daisy and Nancy, as Hardyment points out, develop a friendship that excludes the Swallows.[19] As they explore the "Mango Islands," the last boat to emerge is Daisy and Nancy's: "Both of them were smiling. It seemed to John almost as if they had been glad of the delay" (*SW* 255). It may be that Ransome, good craftsman that he was, intended this merely as a reference to the coming corroboree: but it can equally be seen as a subtle change of direction for Nancy; she is looking elsewhere for friendship.

Dum and Dee are ciphers, while the Mastodon (so called because of the tracks he leaves on the mud with his flat mud-walkers) is another Tom Dudgeon. The "Eels" only convince in maritime matters. The Mastodon can navigate with ease because "he was a pilot on his own ground, and had no need for maps" (*SW*, 178).

But, as is generally agreed, the great "find" of *Secret Water* is Bridget. From the moment that she and Roger are racing each other to eat the porridge so that they can hear the news ("Bridget eyed him balefully and put on speed" [*SW*, 27]). The Ship's Baby proves herself to be a good balance to her family. Roger is no longer the youngest in the family—as he points out when accused of unreliability while blackberrying. As Margery Fisher notes, "Their attitude to the child, their often impatient but genuine affection and concern, tell us something important about all of them.[20] "Oh, well," says her mother. "I suppose you have to grow up some time" (*SW*, 52).

Bridget uses Sinbad (the rescued kitten) as her means of establishing that she has a place in the pecking order. When the Swallows are first surveying Swallow Island, they consider leaving someone to protect the camp, and Bridget, with what is a fresh voice, says that if they see any savages, "We'll send Sinbad at them like a tiger" (*SW*, 74). Her relationship with Titty, in particular, is finely tuned. When they see the others going far away on the surveying expedition, she says, "If we wanted help, they're too far to come," and then she looks "at Titty's face to see how she took this bit of news" (*SW*, 78). Titty is forced to take on responsibility even if she is more nervous than her sister. They see, for example, the prints of the Mastodon in the mud:

> "Horrible?" Bridget looked at the huge prints on the mud and then anxiously over her shoulder.
> "No. Gorgeous," said Titty hurriedly.
> "Oh. Then it's all right," said Bridget.
> "Quite all right," said Titty, though she did not think so. (*SW*, 84)

Likewise, the scene when Titty is trying to decide whether to leave Bridget in the middle of the wade is very reminiscent of the scene in *The River Comes First* where our hero swings himself across the flooded river on a rope.

Establishing herself in the family, especially when she is being protected by both Susan and Titty, brings out a stalwart individuality in Bridget: "'All right, Bridget,' [said Titty]. 'Don't go and cry. Nobody's going to make you a human sacrifice.' 'I think you're beasts,' said Bridget. 'You always make out I'm too young for everything. And now Daddy and Mummy have let me come. They think I'm old enough. And you won't let me be a human sacrifice when somebody wants me'" (*SW*, 107). During the sacrificial dance Bridget shrieks, "'Oh go AWAY. . . . They're just in the middle of it. I don't WANT to be rescued'. . . . 'Don't frighten her,' said Titty. 'I'm *not* frightened,' snapped Bridget" (*SW*, 331, 334).

Secret Water, then, is not, by Ransome's standards, a distinguished book; in a sense, the characters are either too big or too small for the plot. Nevertheless there are many charming period details, such as the telephone number of Miss Powell at Pin Mill ("Woolverstone 30"), and many inspired moments; as when Titty stands in the middle of the Wade: "Titty did not answer. She did not hear him. She was standing between the four posts, the tops of which had been awash when they had sailed through. She was looking straight above her and seeing not hawks or larks or infinite blue sky, but a few feet of swirling water over her head and the red painted bottom and centreboard of a little boat" (*SW*, 278). Another such moment comes when she is looking for a place to rest where "explorers resting tired limbs would not have suddenly to turn into children and get out of the way of some farm cart or other" (*SW*, 288).

Even the ending, tying things up as neatly as the maps are drawn, is saved from the ordinary by Commander Walkers's display of pidgin English: "'Now then,' said the Commander. 'Quick time topside all that. Plenty quick. Bimeby chow chow'" (*SW*, 373).

But, for all its incidental felicities, *Secret Water* is perhaps a rather unsatisfactory book in which to leave the Swallows, who reappear in the sequence in name only in two fantasy novels, *Missee Lee* and *Great Northern?*.

8

Fantastic Voyages: *Peter Duck*, *Missee Lee*, and *Great Northern?*

Ransome's "sequence" of novels is distinguished by using the same nominal characters for two very different purposes. Nine of the twelve novels are "naturalistic," showing, in various ways, characters in "real" settings, developing toward adulthood. Three are romances or fantasies, using, as it were, merely the names or sketches of the characters. The device allows Ransome (and his readers) to indulge the unexploited side of the Swallows' and Amazons' imaginative lives. Not all critics feel that *Great Northern?* should belong to this group; Kit Pearson regards it as the true end of the series, "where there are no more games and where reality itself is an adventure."[1] I would argue that in these three novels, Ransome relies for his effect on action and atmosphere, and to read the characters as having anything other than a nominal relationship with those who develop through the other nine books is to court disappointment. They are merely shadows.

Geoffrey Trease described *all* of Ransome's books as existing in "a fantasy world, disguised under a wealth of realistic detail."[2] This is to define the fantastic very widely, as something out of the ordinary; as the *Shorter Oxford Dictionary* (1987) has it; "Existing only in imagination . . . extravagantly fanciful." Of course, that definition could include *all* fiction. A more common definition today might be more precise: "' Fantasy literature' is a broad term used to describe books in which magic causes impossible, and often wondrous, events to occur."[3] There is, of course, no supernatural magic in Ransome's books, and perhaps the term "romance" ("extravagant fiction . . . wild or wanton exaggeration; a picturesque falsehood" [*SOD*]) would be

124

more appropriate. Yet despite their "wealth of realistic detail," the three books considered here deal with the shadowy area between the improbable and the impossible. They are tales in which the children step beyond their ordinary powers or, in the case of *Great Northern?*, obey the laws of the simplistic world of fiction rather than the complex world of fact.

Ransome himself might have debated the issue in his literary-critical days, but his motto for *Missee Lee* is unsubtle and could apply to all three of the books: "Let it Rip!"[4]

Peter Duck

Ironically, the book that made the Swallows and Amazons series a success is, on the surface, very unlike the primary series. *Peter Duck* (1932) has its ancestry in the pirates-and-treasure books that Stevenson partly parodied and certainly apotheosized in *Treasure Island*. It is a "yarn," that is, a fantasy within a fantasy—a fantasy *of* fictional characters, featuring themselves and epitomizing all the play-acting and small private fantasies that rule the children's minds in the other books.

Peter Duck is a pastiche played with deadpan seriousness and fixed in a recognizably contemporary (that is, 1930s) world. And here, it seems to me, lies its great flaw—a flaw that also underlies, although less obviously, the more fantastic *Missee Lee*. The violence in its great predecessor, *Treasure Island,* is real and ugly, and *Treasure Island,* like much of Stevenson's work, gains immeasurably from the ambiguity that runs through it. The most striking—even admirable—figure in it is Long John Silver: good and bad are blurred.

Kit Pearson identifies the problem very neatly: "Ransome has already created such convincing characters, it is jarring to lift them to another plane of reality."[5] One might say, rather, to another plane of fiction. For the mixing of the 1930s era and black-hearted (and -skinned) pirates produces a curious paradox. On the one hand, the figures of the children's fantasy—Black Jake, Peter Duck, and Bill the cabin boy—are part of a fantasy element that demands a black-and-white outlook: the crew of the *Viper* must be totally evil, otherwise how can we justify their extinction by the waterspout? On the other hand, they must be believable in the context of the contemporary English harbor of Lowestoft. Hence what actually becomes unbelievable is the behavior of the children.

Similarly, the two groups—children and villains—must also be kept well away from each other. Otherwise, what happens when cozy child fantasy and harsh adult fantasy meet?

The attempt to bridge the gap with Bill, the cabin boy, only serves to pinpoint the problem. Bill and Peter Duck are too solidly in the real world of Lowestoft, dealing with the fantasy villains directly; they are very similar to those figures in supernatural fantasy for children (for example, Susan Cooper's "The Dark Is Rising" sequence)[6] who are able to see across a boundary into a different but parallel world. They know what will happen, whereas the others (including Captain Flint) are all playing games.

In a sense, then, the games are unconsciously shown to be trivial, which is emphatically not the case in the "main" sequence of books; and the children are seen to be often helpless. More than once, Captain Flint questions his own judgment—for example, when they are being shot at: "The drunken scoundrels! And us with children aboard!" Peter Duck's laconic reply epitomizes the difficulty: "It was no drunken man that fired that, I'm thinking" (*PD*, 407).

The balance is very precarious, and occasionally Ransome slips: "'I say, Uncle Jim,' said Peggy, 'if the *Viper* does catch us up, what can they really do?' 'They can't do anything,' said Captain Flint. 'Not anything that matters.' Bill opened his mouth and shut it again. Peter Duck looked oddly at Captain Flint, and then glanced round the horizon ahead of them." (*PD*, 405) Well might they look. Bill has just been savagely beaten and kicked by Black Jake and his ruffians and locked into the monkey's cage with his mouth stuffed full of soap. A few moments later, he is shot in the arm. The blurring between the various kinds of fiction is summed up by Susan's casual—even callous—reaction (which is more than a little classist): "And nothing's really gone wrong that can't be mended. . . . Even Bill's arm. Of course, there's his teeth. Were they the second ones or first ones, Bill?" (*PD*, 422).

Occasionally and somewhat uneasily, the narrative voice acknowledges the imbalance. This extract, as John and Nancy are rowing in to try to pick up Captain Flint (who is being pursued by the villains), shows Ransome's intractable problem of reconciling life fiction with fabulous fiction: "Even for Nancy's lurid taste things had been happening too fast. Besides, it was all very well to be the Terror of the Seas, but real pirates, like Black Jake and his friends, were altogether different. Bullies. Cowards and bullies, five of them together going for an old man and a boy" (*PD*, 380). Nancy is so angry that her rowing gets out of time with John's, and she apologizes: "They would have said that if they had got out of time while rowing together on the lake at home. They said it now, though they were rowing at dusk to an island of landslide and earthquake and half-mad pirates roaming about with stolen guns. Still, some things were the same as usual. Wherever you were you said 'Sorry' if you bumped 'stroke' in the back with the bow oar" (*PD*, 381).

The code may still hold, but, in stark contrast with brutality, it may not be adequate. Fortunately, it is not put to the test; but the device of making the children more competent than an adult such as Captain Flint is dangerous. As they pull away from the shore, a rifle shot smashes the lantern. The children are, improbably, fantastically, unconcerned. Nancy says, calmly, "They can't see us now the light's gone. They've got nothing to shoot at. Keep still while I paddle her out" (*PD*, 388).

Peter Duck, far from being a simple, hearty "yarn," is a very ambiguous text—and, it must be said, negatively ambiguous. It draws directly on other traditions, of the sailing-travel book and the wild adventure, and the traditions do not sit well together. Stevenson was successful because Jim Hawkins's world is already distanced, and the moral ambiguities play within that world. The ambiguities and confusions of *Peter Duck* play against the two kinds of characters and the two kinds of actions. For the book to work at all, the reader has to ignore the moral oddities; with *Treasure Island,* they are central to the story. In short, Ransome was at his best when he was at his most original, using these literary sources as secondary, not primary, material.

Nonetheless, the book was a rapid success probably because, unlike *Swallows and Amazons,* it was *not* original. Brogan concurs: "As the readers' constant references to *Treasure Island* show (Arthur had had that book with him in Aleppo [where *Peter Duck* was largely written], and its influence, with that of John Masefield, is all pervasive) it was not really so original as its predecessors. But . . . the familiar Ransome virtues were amply in evidence."[7]

The book, as we have seen, was conceived as a sequel to *Swallows and Amazons,* in which Uncle Jim (Captain Flint) entertains the children during the winter holiday on a trading wherry on the Norfolk Broads. (Hardyment reprints Ransome's laborious first attempt to let the children compose the story themselves.)[8] This evolution is explained in *Swallowdale:* "Peter Duck had grown up gradually to be one of the able-seaman's most constant companions, shared now and then by the boy. . . . He had been the most important character in the story they had made up during those winter evenings in the cabin of the wherry with Nancy and Peggy and Captain Flint. Peter Duck, who said he had been afloat since he was a duckling, was the old sailor who had voyaged with them to the Carribees in the story and, still in the story, had come back to Lowestoft with his pockets full of pirate gold" (*S,* 64).

It is a characteristic touch that the treasure, pragmatically, turns out to be rather faded pearls. But they have still been bought at the cost of a half-dozen lives, not to mention Bill's broken arm and teeth.

Unlike in the "realistic" novels, Ransome in *Peter Duck* can be guilty of what might be called "with-Jack-it-was-the-work-of-a-moment" writing. For example, when Captain Flint and Peter Duck and Bill take the *Wild Cat* out to sea during the combination of tropical storm and earthquake, the description is of the kind that would be laughable in *We Didn't Mean to Go to Sea*: "It had been a desperate night. . . . The *Wild Cat* had been flung over on her beam-ends by the savage squalls. . . . But with the first morning light, Captain Flint had clapped on sail too soon, in his hurry, and a foresail had been split, two jibs had been blown clean out of their ropes, and both topsails, that Mr Duck had begged him not to set, had burst the moment he had them aloft and drawing" (*PD* 359).

Hardyment suggests that the plot and the *Treasure Island* motif were suggested (as Ransome says in *Swallowdale*) by Titty (Altounyan) and by E. F. Knight's *The Cruise of the Alerte* (1890), which Ransome included in "The Mariner's Library" in 1952.[9]

Stevenson, writing about *Treasure Island,* admits that he inadvertently borrowed from Marryat, Kingsley, Washington Irving, and one of Ransome's favorite authors, Defoe. He also stresses, in the same article to which Ransome refers in his letter to the editor of *Junior Bookshelf,* the importance of the map. Ransome's island in *Peter Duck* is a little less ornate than Stevenson's, but it has hills and springs and forests.[10] As Stevenson says, "It is, perhaps, not often that a map figures so largely in a tale, yet it is always important. The author must know his countryside, whether real or imaginary, like his hand; the distances, the points of the compass, the place of the sun's rising, the behavior of the moon, should all be beyond cavil."[11]

The original Ransome elements, though, are perhaps more interesting. Peter Duck himself may be based on Captain Sehmel of *Racundra,* but he owes at least something to Captain Marryat's *Masterman Ready* (1841). As Martin Green observes, "His function is indicated by the name 'Masterman'"; he introduces the principle of social hierarchy even into the . . . adventure setting."[12] In Ransome's world, Peter Duck, the perhaps mythic seaman who is always thinking of the ship ("Begging your pardon, sir . . . the first thing's the ship" [*PD*, 235]), places his social superior but maritime inferior, Captain Flint, in a curious light. At the end of the book, Peter Duck shows little interest in the pearls and is mildly censorious when Captain Flint tries to get him to look at them while he is steering (*PD,* 420). This conflict may be a sublimation of the many arguments and testings of vastly experienced "hand" versus impetuous "master."

He may be quaint ("Duck's my name . . . and Duck's my nature, and I've been afloat as you might say, ever since I were a duckling" [*PD*, 29]) and taciturn, but it is not always clear how far Peter Duck is patronizing the girls and boys who are pretending to be sailors. As to the rest of the cast, they maintain their simple characters, as outlined in the first two novels, except that their slow growth and development is arrested. Titty has less chance to be introspective, Susan more chance to be hyperefficient; Captain Flint is shown to be more impulsive and fallible than before. But otherwise the characters remain ciphers.

Peter Duck is a skillfully written page-turner, a tribute to a very popular genre, with the additional virtue of genuine enthusiasm for maritime matters. But its ambiguities in many ways outweigh its excitements. With *Missee Lee,* the reverse is true.

Missee Lee

"Poor Miss Lee," said Titty.
"Don't know about that," said Captain Flint. "She's got a rum job, but she knows how to do it, and to have a job and know how to do it is one of the best things in this life."[13]

Such is the ultimate moral of Ransome's second, late, fantasy, "starring" the Swallows and Amazons, Captain Flint, and a female Chinese pirate.

If anything, characterization is even more perfunctory than in *Peter Duck. Missee Lee* (1941), like *Secret Water,* is a true series book, in a negative sense. Whereas *The Picts and the Martyrs* is enriched by crossreferences to earlier books, here Ransome is relying on our previous knowledge to supply basic information. Thus nowhere does he explain who all these children are, who Captain Flint is, or, apart from the fact that the book begins at their hundredth port, what they are doing on their world cruise. They are back on the *Wild Cat,* without Peter Duck, in a story told with more dialogue and less technical description than perhaps any other of the books.

At the outset the social/sexist hierarchy is as strong, or even stronger, than ever. Becalmed, and taking measurements with the sextant, only John and Captain Flint understand what is going on. "Nancy knew what some of it meant but could never remember which word meant what." The others, all girls, and the youngest boy "did not even pretend to understand" (*ML,* 26).

Their becalming is very Coleridgean: "They had seen nothing at all but a burning sun by day and blazing stars by night, and water stretching to the horizon" (*ML,* 26). Gibber, Roger's monkey (from *Swallowdale*), drops Captain Flint's cigar into the gasoline tank (a neat collision, or explosion, of symbols), and the characters are cast adrift in the two dinghies *Swallow* and *Amazon.* This romantic circumstance causes Ransome a certain amount of logistic difficulty in getting not only the characters but the two boats back to England.

Even the sea is incidental to the romance: the stormy sea at night is uncomfortable, but not threatening; Susan asks an irritating question about rowing in a gale; John quotes his father and feels better for it; Nancy is still talking about "tame galoots"; Roger constantly (and tiresomely) loses Gibber. When they are being interrogated by Miss Lee, Susan reverts to the Susan of *Swallows and Amazons*: "Suddenly Susan burst out. 'Please, can't we send a telegram to say we're all right?' . . . 'Not just now,' whispered John" (*ML,* 167). Even Captain Flint, when Miss Lee offers him her junk to sail home, is reduced to cliché: "I'd take that little ship anywhere" (*ML,* 278).

Similarly, the children's responses become either routine (in the manner of lesser writers) or competent to the point of unconscious irony. Taicoon Chang, the bird fancier who has formed a bond with Titty, explains, laconically, what might happen to them: " 'To-mollow all plisoners see Missee Lee. All eat man fan with Taicoon. . . . Supper. Perlaps to-mollow no supper. No heads. No wantee chow.' Not very cheering, thought Titty, but the Taicoon did not seem to think it mattered" (*ML,* 131).

All in all, their landfall is reminiscent of the third and fourth books of *Gulliver's Travels,* where Gulliver has become more or less used to being cast ashore, so much so that the act itself becomes rather mundane, and the ultimate security that fantasy brings is emphasized. As Nancy says, "It'll be all right in the end. . . . For Uncle Jim too. It always is" (*ML,* 183)—always, that is, in this kind of book.

But *Missee Lee,* for all that it has been the least popular in terms of sales, has its devotees (it is, for example, Hardyment's favourite Ransome book),[14] and it is easy to see why. From the moment that Susan smells cinnamon on the wind as they near the coast, Ransome is creating a world that owes little to any books in any earlier tradition of children's literature. When Titty cuts a blaze on a tree, "A thick syrup oozed from the bared wood and before she had finished huge blue butterflies were sucking at it," and when they return, the blaze is "covered with dead butterflies and moths drowned in the syrup" (*ML,* 78, 97). They watch a man fishing with cormorants (a very Ransome-ish observation); they see men catching grasshoppers (who provoke a short and significant interchange: Roger says,

LEE RAIL UNDER

"They've got an awful funny smell," and Titty replies, "Just foreign-
ness" [*ML* 111]); and they have lovingly described Chinese meals (at
a time when, it should be remembered, such things were rare in England). Ransome's descriptive skill in picking up details is undiminished, from the sails of the pirate junks ("In some places the sails had
been patched. Flourbags had been used for the patches and it was
odd to read on them the names of English or American millers" [*ML*,
63]) to the details of a shrine. He even glances at the opium-drugged
sailor ("'Pig,' said Nancy" [*ML* 73]). The descriptions in general have
an air of authenticity: "The streets, between the low, green-roofed
houses, were not paved, but just earth trodden smooth. Pigs were
wandering about. There was the harsh trilling of grasshoppers in the
trees. Dust rose about their feet. A big blue butterfly fluttered across
the street above their heads. Here and there women were sitting in
the open doorways. A small boy sitting in the dust and tootling to
himself on a long bamboo flute, took his flute from his lips and stared
at the prisoners as they went by" (*ML*, 150).

As always with Ransome, just as with Defoe, the scene is created
by emphasis on the primary qualities of things; as Inglis puts it, "The
writing . . . is undecorated, and its cadences fix only the scene and
no special attitude towards it."[15] He also made good use of his Chinese
experience of New Year and the Dragon rites, as the Swallows and
Amazons escape in the small dragon: "Lanterns were hanging from
the roof corners of every house, from bamboos stuck out of the windows, from the trees. The noise was like the noise of a battle with the
sharp bangs of the firecrackers which boys and men alike were letting off in all directions. They soon found the other dragons. All three
were dancing and snaking through the streets and in and out among
the houses, with people running beside them with fire-crackers, long
strings of them wound around bamboos, banging, banging, all the
time" (*ML*, 299). Ransome is now making his own myth. *Missee Lee*
may be about pirates, and it may be fantastic, but it is not a pastiche
of earlier books. It is also the only example of his use of his political
experience in children's fiction, for much of the book is concerned
with a power struggle between the three pirate leaders. In *The
Chinese Puzzle,* General Chang Tso-lin is "several inches over six feet
high, a giant among the Chinese" (*CP*, 130) while Taicoon Chang in
Missee Lee is "the tallest man there" (*ML*, 113).

The final escape of Miss Lee is explained by the traditions outlined
in *The Chinese Puzzle*: "A Chinese general is expected to resign as
soon as the position is such as to promise his defeat. He is expected
to keep his wits about him and take sanctuary at the penultimate
move. His enemy will allow him ample time to get away, together
with a decent competence, on the implicit understanding that, should

the position be reversed, a similar *esprit de corps* will produce the same sort of consideration for himself" (*CP*, 122).

Miss Lee's judgment of Captain Flint as "Velly uncultured man" (*ML*, 165), reflects Ransome's assessment of the Chinese view of foreigners, at least in the past. The concept that the Chinese view(ed) foreigners with a mixture of contempt and fear "looks back to the days when the foreigner did indeed present himself to the mind of the peacock-feathered mandarin as a turbulent, greedy-minded hooligan who was strong enough to force mandarins to agree with him in such matters as concerned trading, in which it was below the dignity of a mandarin to take any serious interest . . . [but] foreigners, while intellectually of a low order, had a dreadful power of combining in action" (*CP*, 144–45).

The elements of politics and individuality come together in the eponymous character, and it may well be, as Brogan suggests, that the "secret of the book's appeal is Miss Lee herself." (Ransome's original title for the book was "Poor Miss Lee.")[16]

Missee Lee is an original. "A tiny Chinese woman was sitting on a straight-backed chair. She had a black silk coat and trousers, and gold shoes that rested on a footstool. She was wearing a cartridge belt over her black silk coat, and her fingers were gently tapping a large revolver on her knees" (*ML*, 162). That is her public face, but her private room has easy chairs, an English fireplace, photographs of Cambridge on the mantelpiece, and a hockey stick in the corner. The children have porridge, fried ham and eggs, and Oxford marmalade: "'We always eat Oxford marmalade at Camblidge,' she said. 'Better scholars, better plofessors at Camblidge but better marmalade at Oxford'" (*ML*, 186).

One of the most wry parts of the book is Missee Lee's account of her father's business, which is, in effect, a protection racket in which the Chinese pirates and their victims collude against foreign gunboats, and thence derives the law that no English prisoners should ever be brought to the islands. (It is, of course, the Law of the Jungle once more.) She is nothing if not matter of fact: "Of course they sank junks that had not paid and took plisoners, lich passengers, never poor ones, like your Lobin Hood" (*ML*, 174) Miss Lee's father was "a mandalin, with peacock feather and gold button," and he built up the business, despite transient politics: "He made much money, and Thlee Islands men were happy and contented. Then came the Levolution. Lepublic. Yuan Shih Kai. . . . No matter. Mandalins go. Other men come. We paid the same squeeze and evellything went on as before" (*ML* 172, 174).

Perhaps the most original element is her reason for keeping her prisoners, in defiance of her father's ruling, "like pet rabbits," as

Roger observes (*ML*, 183). For a book of wild adventure to hinge upon
learning classical languages is a bold stroke, producing some mild
ironies: "Even Roger, not very keen on lessons as a rule, finding his
place at the head of the class challenged by John and Captain Flint,
both of whom, brushing up their grammar, were soon hard on his
heels, worked as never in his life and in the evenings was inclined to
protest when other people wanted the use of the dictionary" (*ML*,
234).

But for all there being an element of farce, Ransome takes the basic
motivation of Miss Lee seriously. *Missee Lee* is a much more accomplished book than *Peter Duck*, partly because of its originality and
partly because the "fantastic" characters are given some depth. Missee Lee finally has to face her responsibilities:

> "Thlee Islands," said Miss Lee, talking as if to herself and
> not to her listeners. "Thlee Islands, my father made them
> one. He tlusted me to keep them one. And now I make them
> thlee again. The counsellor is light. Better to have no En-
> glish students, no English plisoners, no Camblidge, but keep
> Thlee Islands one, and my father happy in his glave."
> "Are you going to let us go?" said Roger. . . .
> Miss Lee flashed for a moment into anger. "You all velly
> pleased. Even Loger."
> "We've loved being here," said Nancy. "We'll remember it
> all our lives."
> "Short lives," said Miss Lee. "Plobably velly short lives."
> (*ML*, 275–76)

It also seems, with the flexibility of Captain Flint even more on
display than usual, that Ransome is far more in control of the para-
doxes of the blending of the two kinds of fantasy.

If the thinness of the characterization of the children in *Missee Lee*
is compensated for by the pace and color of the book, the same cannot
be said of the last, and, sadly, least of the books, *Great Northern?*.

Great Northern?

Hugh Brogan, describing *Great Northern?* (1947), sums it up very
neatly: "The subject . . . verges on the melodramatic; the plot . . .
seems to be an uneasy conflation of the mode of *Peter Duck* with that
of *Coot Club*; and indeed the . . . theme is too like that of *Coot Club*
for comfort. Ransome has little or nothing new to say about the children's characters. But he knows his business, and by infinite atten-

tion to detail makes his commonplace tale solidly interesting and convincing."[17]

The subject matter, and much of the plot, was suggested to him by a friend. The dedication of the book, "To Myles North, who, knowing a great deal of what happened, asked me to write the whole story" has often been taken as a punning joke; it is not. Myles North supplied him with feathers of the vulturine guinea-fowl for fly-tying (an episode described and illustrated in *Mainly about Fishing*) and, being an enthusiast for the Swallows and Amazons, also provided a detailed synopsis of what came to be *Great Northern?*.[18]

Although there are brilliant episodes, the plot is contrived, and the characters are required to be far more insensitive and gauche than ever before. Brogan points out that "By the time of *Great Northern?* Nancy and John are allegedly about sixteen. Yet they show no signs of emerging from childhood";[19] indeed, these shadowy figures seem to have regressed. They all become less shrewd and cruder: Nancy more childish and manic ("Great Gannets and Guillemots!"),[20] Dorothea more protective of Dick; Dick far more unconfident; Peggy a simpleton ("He'll find things out from Peggy. . . . She's simply bound to blurt everything out if he asks her. . . . She's always ready to chatter to anyone" [*GN*, 146]); John more the elder brother than ever, and much more sharp-tongued ("'Gosh!' said Roger. 'I wish I'd been there.' 'You wouldn't have done any better,' said John. 'Probably worse'" [*GN*, 147]). Roger himself, now once again small-boy-and-engines, loses his intelligence ("'You ought to have used the engine coming out of harbour. . . .' 'And told the *Pterodactyl* just what we were doing,' said John. 'I forgot that,' said Roger. 'Sorry'" [*GN*, 157]).

Only rarely is even Captain Flint anything like his old self. Sitting at the cross-trees, he sees the children being apprehended, and he "banged his fist on the cross-trees. Never, never again, would he take children with him for a cruise. [Note his view of "children" as lesser and other.] He hurt his fist but hardly felt it. He had a sudden vision of indignant mothers" (*GN*, 294).

Ransome is now a long way from the uncluttered vision of childhood. In *Great Northern?* he shifts his viewpoint more widely than ever before, and this technique serves only to emphasize the lack of sympathy with his characters. They can survive in their innocent world only by being viewed close up. Seen in perspective, they become subject to the laws of the real world, and hence must be expected to grow, and this fantasy, although clothed in realistic clothes, does not allow that.

Much of the plot depends on the irritating (and, in the context of the series, inadmissible) device, common to inferior books for children, of disbelief between peers and adults. In one case, John actually becomes sarcastic—"Dick's got some sense. . . . How many savage Gaels did you see, Dick, scientifically speaking?" (*GN*, 91)— and when the question arises again, as well it might, it is inconvenient to the plot development. Captain Flint starts to ask about the "savage Gaels" but "himself brushed that idea aside before anybody had time to answer" (*GN*, 139).

Even the shape of the plot has changed; the book has, very noticeably, an abstract beginning and end. It begins with a glimpse of an outside observer, the highland boy, whose attitude to what is to follow immediately reduces its stature: "On a hill above the cliff a boy in highland dress turned from watching the deer in the valley to look out over the sea. He saw a sail far away. It was no more than a white speck in the distance and presently he turned his back on it and settled down again to watch the deer" (*GN*, 11).

At the end, without comment, the last page shows the same boy watching the ship, the *Sea Bear,* sailing away. In some ways, the ending may be seen symbolically as the culmination of Ransome's gradual break with psychological closure. *Great Northern?* begins in the Scottish islands, and it ends there; whereas even the exotic *Missee Lee* begins in a friendly port and ends in the English harbor of St. Mawes. But the shape of the text is an adult one, and it jars with the childishness of the characters. *Great Northern?* has, consequently, a feel of not being related to the rest of the sequence at all. The *Times Literary Supplement* writer, who had suggested that Ransome generally followed classical tragedy in placing the climax in Act 4, noted the deviation. "When he departs from this scheme in *Great Northern?* and puts the climax at the very end the reader feels cheated."[21]

Yet the climax is skillful and passionate, and the details of sailing and bird-watching and photography as fascinating as ever. The idea of making a hide (for photographing the birds) out of netting, for which one has first to make the netting needles (*GN*, 181), is characteristically Ransome, as are the details of the folding boat, putting the *Sea Bear* on legs, and so on. Even the deer lore moves us into new areas of interest, although it is an area that reflects badly on the intelligence of the protagonists. Ian, the Scottish boy, contemplates the *Sea Bear*: "Angus had told him what they were up to. Deer are like salmon. They come back to the places where they began their lives, and by shifting the hinds in the breeding season a dishonest man could ruin his neighbour's deer-forest and improve his own without ever laying a hand on a single beast. It was the very meanest of tricks. And to use children for the driving made it meaner" (*GN*, 199). This external viewpoint is reminiscent of the loss of poise in *Peter Duck.* The children—referred to as children rather than being the central, respected figures—are reduced to a subservient role, to inferior beings. They are actually caught in wrongdoing (and the fact that it comes of ignorance does not constitute an excuse in the code); they are patronized even by their contemporaries. They are no longer in control or even particularly admirable.

Taken at its lowest level, *Great Northern?* has its strengths. Mr. Jemmerling, the egg collector (who runs a motorboat and wears plus-fours and pink pajamas at sea), is a splendid villain, quite clearly beyond the pale. But even with him, the effectiveness of the scenes depends on artificiality, such as stagey dialogue or the requirement that the clever Dick be very slow on the uptake.

The book does have a remarkable ending, with Ransome's two perhaps most sympathetic characters returning the eggs of the harassed Great Northern Divers to the nest, while the Swallows, the Amazons, and the rest fade away. The last words of Nancy are the courteous bowing-out of "All right, Professor. . . . Your eggs"; the last of John are "Boat's ready." Then, "a moment later [note the cliché] they were both afloat. Dick was rowing as quietly as he could. Titty was sitting in the stern nursing the egg-box. The crew of the *Sea-Bear* still on the shore, the McGintys, father and son, Captain Flint, the raging egg-collector and his man, watched by the dogs and ghillies, all had ceased to exist for them. Nothing mattered now but the birds" (*GN*, 347).

And so the book ends, on an optimistic note certainly and on a note of closure for the birds; but the characters are still in motion. Titty, the mystic, and ("blinking joyfully through his spectacles" [*GN*, 351]) Dick, Ransome's inner alter ego (as opposed to John and Captain Flint, who are, as it were, his outer images), are rowing back to tell the others. The ending is a triumph of technique over material, and Ransome had taken the series as far as (and perhaps farther than) it could reasonably go.

9

The Achievement of Arthur Ransome

Even with the benefit of hindsight, it is not easy to judge the influence of a writer. Geoffrey Trease, himself one of the innovators of children's books in the 1930s, has pointed out that at the time he "did not know that . . . Ransome . . . had blazed a new trail with a book called *Swallows and Amazons*."[1]

Children's books were not critically respectable at the time. The Carnegie Medal was not established by the British Library Association until 1936 (Ransome thought that the publicity was so inadequate that "it would have been better to send the blessed thing by post");[2] the first list of recommended books for children was produced by the National Book Council in 1938. Gillian Avery, an authority on nineteenth-century children's books, recalls her childhood reading in the 1930s: "It was possible then for the bookish child to be far less self-conscious in his [sic] choice of reading than he is in the 1970s. . . . The books that were being written for us during that period were in general an uncharted sea, and we were considered as capable of making our way through it as anybody else."[3]

Because there was little knowledge "about" children's books, they had little status. Even as late as 1948, the academic world's opinion of writing for children was brought home, rather painfully, to Ransome. Brogan writes of his going to Durham University to receive an honorary degree: "Only when Arthur appeared at the ceremony did he discover that he was going to receive only an honorary MA, not being judged worthy of anything higher by the then Professor of English, one Abbott. To make matters worse, he discovered that Edith Sitwell was to get an honorary doctorate at the same ceremony, and he must have found it hard to see that she had any higher claims than his."[4]

By the time of his death, Ransome was a national figure and his books classics. Children's literature, even if it had not attained the critical respectability that it has today, was, in terms of numbers and quality, going through a second "golden age." Ransome's contribution to this change is best seen in terms of the context surrounding children's literature when he began writing and of his personal achievement and influence, both specific and general.

Conventional readings of the history of British children's literature suggest six periods. From the mid-eighteenth century until the second decade of the nineteenth century, writing for children was predominantly religious and didactic. In Victorian times, there was a tendency toward greater realism in the domestic story (usually aimed at girls) and a more robust portrayal of children in general. For boys, morals were carried by epic empire-building and sea stories, often in the tradition of the "Robinsonnade," usually featuring extravagant adventures and cardboard characters. The boys' school story, almost invariably carrying a strongly stated moral purpose in shaping the "manly boy," developed in parallel.

The period from the publication of *Alice in Wonderland* (1865) and *The Water Babies* (1863) until the outbreak of World War I in 1914 has been seen as the first Golden Age of children's books. While both religious/domestic and "empire-building" stories were still dominant, an increasing number of writers were shifting the viewpoint of their writing from the adult controlling consciousness to the point of view of the child. (A classic individual example of this transition is Kenneth Grahame, even in his writing for adults.)

The child in children's books became both more self-motivated and more respected. The children in Edith Nesbit's books, whether in her domestic series about the Bastable family or in the fantasies such as *The Phoenix and the Carpet,* are recognizable children with strong family loyalties. The books do not carry a freight of moral lessons. The children were still bounded, however, by a closed, nursery-oriented world, and even in Nesbit (perhaps the most politically aware of them all) there is a strong, if unconscious, classism. As Leeson points out, in general, "Always in the background, to be the butt of 'ragging' or to clear up the mess when the pranks are over, is the anonymous figure of the servant."[5] Nonetheless, Nesbit, as Lancelyn Green puts it, "carried the child-novel right out into the Spring sunshine once and for all." Her influence was immense, although "surprisingly few child-novels followed hers that win anywhere near the status of classics . . . until Arthur Ransome produced *Swallows and Amazons.*"[6]

Nonetheless, children in the 1920s and 1930s had the legacy of writers such as George MacDonald, Louisa May Alcott, Frances Hodgson Burnett, Kenneth Grahame, Beatrix Potter, and J. M. Barrie, while the undergrowth of literature gradually absorbed the empire-building stories and the school story. In the early years of the century, Kipling had effectively brought realism to the school story in *Stalky and Co.,* contributed very individualistically to the animal story in *Just So Stories* and *The Jungle Books,* and celebrated the English countryside and empire in *Puck of Pook's Hill* and *Rewards and Fairies.* Even earlier, Richard Jefferies, in *Bevis, the Story of a Boy,* although it is essentially a book *about* childhood rather than one *for* the child, brought together the solid principles of rectitude and self-sufficiency (the "stiff-upper-lip" qualities) and translated them into a childhood context. He also "liberated" the children, acknowledged the anarchy inherent in the child, and celebrated a specific place. As we have seen, he also made good use of the literary tradition of the nineteenth century.

Stevenson, similarly, while making full use of the adventure "yarn" conventions, had introduced moral ambiguity into the children's book. This attitude contrasted with the concept of a simplistic conformist code, which is demonstrated throughout Kipling, and which, as part of the public-school ethos, suffuses both the "quality" books of the period and the popular press.

The Golden Age, because of its liberation of the imagination and of the book itself, opened the way for mass-market production. Despite Kipling's demolition of the school story in *Stalky and Co.,* George Orwell, in his famous attack on boys' stories in 1940, found them "sodden" with the worst principles of the empire-building days,[7] and even the girls' school story, as Cadogan and Craig point out, "flourished between the wars, when old values and traditions were being reasserted in a new guise."[8] More problematic was the influence of sentimentality, epitomized, perhaps, by A. A. Milne, whose "Pooh" books, although best-sellers of the 1920s and thereafter, are for at least some of the time an adult's view of childhood.

But opinions of this period vary greatly. In 1932, the *Library Association Review* described output for children as "a few admirable books, submerged in an ocean of terrible trash . . . unreal school stories, impossible adventure, half-witted fairy tales . . . in every respect disgraceful."[9] Eleanor Graham, writing of 1927, says that there was "no reviewing. . . . by and large [children's books] were regarded as trash. . . . No one, of course, would stop to consider critically the work of Angela Brazil . . . but there were many people then who assumed that *all* children's books were on that level."[10] The fat, bulky "rewards" dominated the market: "[Rewards] were written according to one of several approved formulae, illustrated often with a splendid disregard for subject-matter (the pictures were often re-used in different contexts). . . . It was . . . virtually impossible for any story of literary or sociological value to be produced in this machine."[11] Authors were paid small amounts for the outright sale of copyrights.

The vast majority of children's reading was from the nineteenth century, and, as Trease observes, "A new story in 1920 or 1930 tended to be a fossil in which one could trace the essential characteristics of one written in 1880 or 1890."[12] Perhaps not surprisingly, then, Ransome's publisher, Jonathan Cape, did not at first show much interest in *Swallows and Amazons*: "He agreed to publish *Rod and Line* and, after Arthur had told him something of *Swallows,* that too, for an advance of a hundred pounds. 'But it's the essays we want.'"[13]

Ransome himself in the *Autobiography* fulminates against what he calls "imitation" books, a view perhaps particularly appropriate to the period when he began to write for children himself: "These 'books' cost their authors nothing to produce and can be turned out at high speed. They do not, as a real book does, become part of a reader's inmost life" (*A,* 35–36).

Ransome did not revolutionize this situation single-handed. Hugh Crago quotes Sheila Ray's observation that "there was not a whole lot happening in children's fantasy in the 1930s" and comments, "In fact there was not much happening in children's literature, period. In England, what *was* happening was Arthur Ransome's 'Swallows and Amazons' series."[14] This is a pardonable exaggeration. As Crouch admits, Ransome was not alone: "Numerically, the thirties were the most productive years of the century; more interesting authors made their first appearance even than in the decade of E. Nesbit. It was notably an age of professional writing."[15] Publishers were expanding and creating children's book departments, and the BBC began its "Children's Hour" radio program in 1936.

Indeed, in spite of the "imitation" books, a list of Ransome's contemporaries and immediate predecessors is undeniably impressive. The twenties had seen Basil Blackwell's experimental *Joy Street* series (1923–26), with writers like Walter de la Mare, Eleanor Farjeon, and Rose Fyleman. Hugh Lofting began writing in 1920 and Richmal Crompton in 1922; Masefield published his fantasy *The Midnight Folk* in 1928 and *The Box of Delights* in 1935. There were Ardizzone's *Little Tim and the Brave Sea Captain* (1936), Jean de Brunhoff's *Babar the Elephant* (1934), and Hale's *Orlando the Marmalade Cat* (1938), while Dr. Seuss's *And to Think That I Saw It on Mulberry Street* came to England in 1939. Characters such as Barbara Euphan

Todd's Worzel Gummidge (1936), P. L. Travers's Mary Poppins (1934), Tolkien's Hobbit (1937), and Alison Uttley's Little Grey Rabbit (1929) made their first appearances. There were books with social consciences, such as Trease's Bows against the Barons (1934) and Eve Garnett's Family from One End Street (1937); the first "career" books, such as Noel Streatfeild's Ballet Shoes (1936); and classics such as T. H. White's The Sword in the Stone (1938). All these books are still in print. But as Crouch says, "Predominantly . . . this was an age of naturalism, the master of which was Arthur Ransome."[16]

In many ways Ransome was a man of his time: he wrote of a family structure and a moral code that were essentially late Victorian; he tapped into a literary tradition that was essentially nineteenth century; he followed Nesbit, Kipling, and Carroll in according his child characters the respect that they would have accorded themselves; and his settings were basically well-to-do middle class.

What, then, were the individual qualities of his writing? To a large extent, this book has been a celebration of these qualities, and, as his imitators showed, his contribution was a unique combination of virtues. His prose style is verb centered; his focalizers are 95 percent children. His plot structures derive from the fairy-tale and evolve through the series so that they represent a bildungsroman for the child reader who follows them through. His characters are either members of intimate societies that readers can enter (the Swallows), or fallible characters with whom readers can empathize (the D.'s), or energetic figures whose games and enthusiasms readers can share (the Amazons). Perhaps most of all, he was an enthusiast, and enthusiasts are generally childlike in their devotion to a single cause and purpose and their absorption in every practical detail; they give everything equal weight, equal respect.

So to say that Ransome wrote "realistically" is not simply to say that he wrote about practical, or "outdoor" matters—although he did, of course, make a great stride in this direction. (Roger Lancelyn Green describes Swallows and Amazons as "the apotheosis of outdoor adventure, the realization towards which Mark Twain and Jefferies and Thompson Seton were all groping.")[17] What he did do was to write about skills as equal to equal, regardless of the expertise required. As Landsberg points out, "When I finally had a chance to sit at the tiller of a dinghy, I knew the heft, the feel and the arcane language as though I were a secret inhabitant of a nautical world. As, indeed, I was."[18]

The point most frequently made about Ransome is that he virtually "invented" the holidays in fiction. In Pigeon Post, when the Swallows meet each other, fresh from their various (boarding) schools, there is a notable exchange: "'Hullo,' said John and Susan. 'Hullo,' said Titty and Roger. . . . Term time was gone as if it had been wiped out. Real life was beginning again" (*PP*, 26). Certainly, school is hardly mentioned. Some critics have suggested that Ransome was merely reflecting a trend, and that the whole genre of the holiday story "is perhaps itself a cultural by-product of the social institution of the annual holiday as it emerged in the late nineteenth century."[19] But Ransome is concentrating on the free time of the child, not on the fact of the holiday. There are only rare references to school, and apart from *Swallows and Amazons,* none of the books ends with any indication that a return to school is a threatening fact on the immediate horizon.

In substituting the Lake District or the Norfolk Broads for the confines of the family garden, or the (diminishing) empire, Ransome has liberated his children while still retaining a sense of scale. Family ties are not broken; the emphasis has merely changed. Children operate within both a landscape and a code that have real meanings. Simultaneously, he allows male and female to work together, to break the bonds of conventional roles.

This is not to say, as we have seen, that he does this comprehensively. Nancy Blackett, as "tomboy," is essentially a type; only in *We Didn't Mean to Go to Sea* does Susan escape her domesticity. Ransome can well be accused of being sexist, for merely to reflect things as they are, by the very virtue of writing a book, to reinforce them. However, it can be argued that in things of the soul (and of the code)—the things that really matter not only to Ransome's characters but to his child readers—gender is unimportant. John and Titty, for example, opposites in temperament and ambition, are closest in their understanding of the unspoken.

Similarly, Ransome's democracy, although it does not ignore the trappings of class, is really concerned with something else: mutual respect gained by mutual interest. Thus the Amazons may have cook and occasional chauffeur, but they are, in Ransome's scale of things, not superior to the farmboy, Jacky. As Inglis points out, "the greatness of Arthur Ransome's best novels has very little to do with the children in them being at private school and possessing . . . spare cash."[20] This is, in a sense, the democracy of childhood. It has not mattered to generations of child readers that these characters possess family or playthings that are beyond their reach. What is important, from the child's point of view, is the essence: the trappings are peripherals. Because most of Ransome's books, although not "fantasies," sit (increasingly) apart from the "real" world, what might otherwise be seen as indoctrinating elements can be seen as dialectical. From the problems that Ransome has in mixing genres (in, for example, *Peter Duck*) one can see that his readers' awareness of the difference between life and fiction is integral to the construction of the stories.

In a sense, the "liberal" Ransome presents not so much an ideal world in which children can play, but a world of ideals to which his readers can aspire: a world of equality and respect. Here his great achievement lies, even though he will be as much remembered, and most directly imitated, for the attractive surface features of his novels.

Swallows and Amazons, observes Carpenter in the *Oxford Companion to Children's Literature,* "was indirectly responsible for a great deal of undistinguished hack-work."[21] I would say rather that *Swallows and Amazons* was directly responsible for the hack work, and *indirectly* responsible for much of what is best in British children's literature. When writers tried to replicate the "Ransome formula," they tended to follow surface features—families, on holiday, practicing some skill—which, as we have seen, were attractive but not fundamental to the Ransome "mix." The "formula," if it can be so called, was too complex to be imitated in all its subtlety.

Therefore it is difficult to pinpoint Ransome's earliest imitators. Certainly M. E. Atkinson's *August Adventure* has many of the ingredients and is distinguished by its portrayal of family relationships.[22] But the more interesting (and flattering for Ransome) was *The Far-Distant Oxus* by Katharine Hull and Pamela Whitlock.

First published in 1937, in a format identical to the Ransome novels (except that the binding was red with black lettering rather than green with gold lettering), the manuscript was sent to Ransome by two schoolgirls ("Katherine is 15, Pam is 16").

Ransome described how it came to be written and published in an extensive introduction to the book, which perhaps unwittingly displays a not-too-admirable aspect of his character. He first suspected it of being a hoax: "In fact, since 1933, when some of the secrets of a young novelist called Dorothea were given away in a book called *Winter Holiday,* a good many of the letters I have received have ended with the words 'P.S.—I am writing a book.' Alas, it is easy to begin writing a book. The difficult thing is to keep it up."[23] Accordingly, he suspected the girls' names as disguising "some wretched grown-up masquerading behind them and trying to make me the victim of a hoax" (*FD,* 11).

This does not say much for Ransome's literary perception, for, as he says later, that readers will find, "with delight, that they are reading something different from any grown-up book. . . . [The authors] are not old enough to be afraid of their youth. . . . For them the dew

AT THE BECKFOOT GATE

is still on the grass. . . .The book is alive from beginning to end with looking and seeing and feeling. . . . This book is exactly what its authors, being children, wanted to read, and it could not have been written by anyone older than themselves" (*FD*, 16–18).

Fortunately, Ransome made up for his cynicism by adopting the book and seeing it through the press. He recounts a famous story of taking the manuscript to his publisher, Jonathan Cape: "'I've got this year's best children's book under my arm,' I told him. 'When did you get it finished?' he politely replied. 'It's not mine at all,' I said, and told him what I have just told you" (*FD*, 13).

And, of course, *The Far-Distant Oxus* is only partly an imitation. One of the rare books by children and for children, it is full of the kind of details that Ransome has a reputation for giving, but which in fact he universalizes. Hull and Whitlock's children do not eat, as in Ransome, anonymous steak and kidney puddings; they eat, not simply sausages, but "Sainsbury's best Paris sausages straight from the frying-pan so that there would be fewer greasy plates to wash up" (*FD*, 115).

Almost everything about *The Far-Distant Oxus* is in some sense awkward from a purist's point of view—the characterization, the occasionally melodramatic incidents, and, notoriously, the building of the hut (with windows) Peran-Wisa, in an afternoon (*FD*, 77–79). But this is constantly compensated for by charm, energy, and very clear-eyed observation. At the Village Sports, there is a marquee: "There were enormous marrows that looked too tough to be eaten by anyone. . . . Among the classes of fruit there was a competition for melons that had only four entries, and Jennifer felt miserably sorry for the poor person who was the only one not to win a prize. Surely the judges could give a fourth, just for once. . . . Farther on there were winning rosebuds looking rather lonely all by themselves in glass pots" (*FD*, 205).

The love of horses replaces Ransome's love of sailing, with, to the uninitiated, a similar tone of obscurantism; and, as has often been observed, there is a latent sexuality (especially in the descriptions of Maurice) that is totally absent from Ransome. Very instructively bridging the generations, Maurice bears some comparison to the hero of another book by a teenaged authoress, Ponyboy in S. E. Hinton's *The Outsiders*. Maurice in *The Far-Distant Oxus* is described thus: "A boy of about fourteen, tall and dark and lithe, stood holding a coal black pony. A Labrador stood alert at his side" (*FD*, 14). Similarly, when Anthony swims in the lake (whose waters are like "dilute golden syrup"), matters are touched on that never appear in the "Swallows and Amazons" volumes: "He flung off his Aertex shirt and shorts. . . . He debated whether to climb on [the raft] . . . but decided that the owners of the hideous house might be unduly shocked if they looked out of their bedroom window and saw a nude boy propelling himself across their lake" (*FD,* 246). Ransome's recognition of this remarkable book says a good deal for his empathy with children.

But what of the lesser imitators, following other features of Ransome's books? Sheila Ray, writing on Enid Blyton, noted that following *Swallows and Amazons,* "by 1938, when . . . Blyton made her first contribution to the genre . . . the pattern was well established. . . . A mixed group of boys and girls . . . parents . . . removed to the fringe of the action. . . . Events took place during . . . one holiday, given shape by the regional setting and by an interest in a hobby or sport."[24] But the majority of imitations (however flattering) were in the vein of Marjorie Lloyd's *Fell Farm Holiday,* commissioned by Kaye Webb for the Puffin imprint in 1951. The first book has a nice air of probability, and a fairly original touch in having each chapter narrated by one of the five children in the family. Beyond that, little more need be said of it than to quote the "blurb," which, in both style and content, is a travesty of Ransome's work:

> This is one of those jolly holiday stories which almost make you feel you've been there. There were five of the Brownes, two pairs of twins, and young Sally, the odd man out. They nearly always spent their long holidays in the Lake District and on this occasion they went without their parents. They always stayed at the same farm, high up in the hills, where they knew every animal on the place and the country round. They made a "hide" and spent days bird watching. They did some hard climbing, camped out in the hills, and had a first-rate mixture of fun and adventure.[25]

Another writer to have the temerity to use Ransome's Lake District was Geoffrey Trease, who specialized in rescuing worn genres. In *No Boats on Bannermere* (1949),[26] the absent element is the family, and although the characters do develop, the emphasis is upon the action, which is often routine. As Trease said, the books were inspired when two Cumbrian schoolgirls asked him "why there were no day-school stories about children like themselves."[27] Perhaps in the postwar world, such mechanistic inspirations were more the norm.

Peter Dawlish and Aubrey de Selincourt managed to capture some of the sailing ethos but often had to fall back on conventional "children's book" materials. Dawlish (a professional sailor) is the lesser writer, but he clearly shared many of Ransome's feelings. *"Dauntless" Takes Recruits,* for example, ends with a recognizable sentiment: "Then leave that stinking engine. . . . We need your weight on the halyard."[28] Aubrey de Selincourt, some of whose books were illustrated in Ransome style by Guy de Selincourt, borrows both the family and Peter Duck, in the shape of "Uncle Bob," called "The Bosun." Nonetheless, *Family Afloat*, especially, has some strongly atmospheric writing and a restrained love of boats and sailing.[29]

A somewhat ironic testimony of Ransome's influence is found in Elisabeth Mace's grim post-apocalypse novel, *Ransome Revisited* (1975), in which a group of children fleeing across a savage England find a copy of *Swallowdale*. They read it in disbelief that life could have been so happy: "a book . . . that tells what it was like, before our time."[30] But the book is lost, and with it the idyllic life it portrayed.

"Every writer of stories of adventure in the open-air since 1930 has owed a debt to Ransome."[31] It may well be that Ransome's influence is wider than that, partly, at least because of his professionalism and integrity. He demonstrated that children's books did not need to be written to a formula or to depart from the norms of possibility.

(Of course, those norms are a movable feast. In Mary Treadgold's novel about wartime life on the German-occupied Channel Islands, *We Couldn't Leave Dinah* [1941] one of the characters observes: "Just think how the Arthur Ransome children would dote on it.")[32]

He also took activities seriously, so seriously that it was possible for him to integrate their accomplishment into the novels without the necessity (with very rare exceptions) for overtly didactic asides. He suggested the possibilities of books that were true to families and to family codes; that acknowledged the importance of family relationships and the dignity of the child; that established the importance of *place*.

But perhaps most of all, as L. A. G. Strong noted in 1940, Ransome "never writes down. . . . [He] always assumes an active and enquiring intelligence in his readers."[33] It is a point that reviewers have often made. The *Times Literary Supplement* wrote in 1934: "Perhaps his success as a writer for young people is due to the fact that he takes his readers more seriously than the authors of most 'juveniles' do; for in reality he is a children's novelist, and has the peculiar quality of being able to reveal children to themselves."[34] *Books,* in 1942, observed that he used "adult fiction technique . . . to develop a story from a young person's point of view."[35]

Postwar children's literature has been the richer for his example. Certainly hack work has persisted and, indeed, has moved into new areas that Ransome would have disliked; but the "mainstream" children's novel is of a generally higher standard than before.

There is, however, one writer who is close to Ransome in all his characteristics except two: style and output. William Mayne has written around a hundred children's books of virtually every genre (*except* small-boat sailing). But his novels have a respect for skills and craft, a capacity to evoke place (very often Yorkshire, across the Pennine hills from Ransome's Lake District), and a remarkable use of family dialect.

And what of Ransome's future reputation? Fisher feels that "Ransome's genius as a story-teller is not likely to be fully recognised until his books are read as period pieces . . . so that their social and emotional content are seen in proportion and not as awkward or incomprehensible *alternatives* to the world of today."[36] If that is true, it is, I think, also true that for many readers his books are already read in this way. For others, what were once "realistic" novels have become "fantasy" already, and they can be read as such, so that the central values and themes come directly to the reader.

There are, admittedly, certain problems with Ransome. The fact that he does not deal with sex at all has raised questions (largely with adults) about his place in the age ranges. The greater freedom in certain directions, the weakening of "family" ties, wider secondary experiences, have all tended to lower the "appropriate" reading age. Set against this is the unusual length of his books, while the pace seems increasingly unfashionable. Even more unfashionable—to the regret, perhaps, of many adults—may be the moral codes.

Although Ransome has none of the racist faults that have cast doubts on the writings of Lofting and Blyton, there may yet be problem over *Missee Lee*. "I hope," Landsberg notes, "that the pidgin English spoken by the Chinese pirates doesn't ban *Missee Lee* from current book lists . . . so dogmatic have we become about culturally correct attitudes."[37] (Surprisingly, Ransome's two uses of the word "nigger," in *Peter Duck* and *The Big Six,* were allowed to stand by his British publishers in recent "revised" editions; he seems to have used the word as an acceptably descriptive, rather than discriminatory, adjective.)

But for all that, Ransome's classic status—which, in British children's books at least, means that he is handed down from generation to generation—will ensure that he is read; and once he is read, his many virtues as a writer seem likely to ensure his reputation.

In 1930, introducing the book to American readers, Ransome wrote that in writing *Swallows and Amazons,* "I began to understand that in writing about children one is writing about one's own childhood as well as theirs, and so, in a way, about childhood in general." One of the main pleasures of the book, for him, was "the way in which the children in it have no firm dividing line between make-believe and reality, but slip in and out of one and the other again and again and backwards and forwards, exactly as I had done when I was a child and, as I rather fancy, we all of us do in grown-up life."[38]

He was very modest about his achievements; writing, again for American children, in 1935: "It seems to me that in writing books for boys and girls I have the best of my growing-up years over again and the best of being old as well, which is a very great deal more than I deserve."[39]

Perhaps a fitting ending, summing up Ransome's attitudes, would be the words that he wrote on a cutting from the *Listener* of his article on Isaac Walton[40] (now in the Brotherton collection of the University of Leeds): "There is no duty we so much underrate as the duty of being happy."

Notes and References

Preface

1. *Swallows and Amazons* (1930; new illustrated ed., London: Jonathan Cape, 1931); hereafter cited in the text as *SA*.
2. Fred Inglis, *The Promise of Happiness: Value and Meaning in Children's Fiction* (Cambridge, England: Cambridge University Press, 1981), 129.
3. Frank Eyre, *British Children's Books in the Twentieth Century* (London: Longman, 1971), 94.
4. Marcus Crouch, *Treasure Seekers and Borrowers: Children's Books in Britain, 1900–1960* (London: Library Association, 1962), 72.
5. B. E. Todd, review of *Swallows and Amazons, Spectator,* 13 September 1930, 358.
6. Hugh Brogan, *The Life of Arthur Ransome* (London: Jonathan Cape, 1984), 336.
7. "A Letter to the Editor," *Junior Bookshelf,* 1, no. 4 (1937); reprinted in Marcus Crouch and Alec Ellis, eds., *Chosen for Children* (London: Library Association, 1977), 6.
8. Ibid.
9. Kit Pearson, "Arthur Ransome, 1884–1967," in Jane Bingham, ed., *Writers for Children* (New York: Charles Scribner's Sons, 1987), 456.

Chapter One

1. *AA Illustrated Guide to Britain* (London: Drive Publications, 1979), 374, 376.
2. *Young Wings,* Junior Literary Guild, September 1935, 7.
3. *The Autobiography of Arthur Ransome* (London: Jonathan Cape, 1976), 28; hereafter cited in the text as *A.*
4. Hugh Shelley, *Arthur Ransome,* Bodley Head Monograph (London: Bodley Head, 1960), 40.
5. "A Hundred Years of Children's Books" (review of Roger Lancelyn Green's *Tellers of Tales*), *Spectator,* 4 December 1953.
6. Brogan, *Life,* 7–8.
7. Marcus Crouch and Alec Ellis (eds.), *Chosen for Children,* (London: Library Association, 1977), 7–8.
8. *See* Lois Kuznets, *Kenneth Grahame* (Boston: Twayne, 1987), 5–6.

9. *Young Wings,* 7.

10. Brogan, *Life,* 49.

11. *The Souls of the Streets and Other Little Papers* (London: Brown, Langham, 1904), 11, 31, 44.

12. *The Stone Lady: Ten Little Papers and Two Mad Stories* (London: Brown, Langham, 1905).

13. Quoted by Rupert Hart-Davis in the Introduction to *Bohemia in London,* illus. Fred Taylor (London: Chapman and Hall, 1907; Oxford University Press, 1984), xiii; hereafter cited in the text as *BL.*

14. Brogan, *Life,* 55.

15. *A History of Storytelling: Studies in the Development of Narrative* (London, T. C. and E. C. Jack, 1909), viii; hereafter cited in the text as *HS.*

16. *Edgar Allan Poe: A Critical Study* (London: Martin Secker, 1910), x; hereafter cited in the text as *P.*

17. *The Book of Friendship: Essays, Poems, Maxims and Prose Passages* (London: T. C. and E. C. Jack, n.d. [1909]), prefatory pages.

18. *The Book of Love: Essays, Poems, Maxims and Prose Passages* (London: T. C. and E. C. Jack, n.d. [1909]), prefatory pages.

19. *The Hoofmarks of the Faun* (London: Martin Secker, 1911), 133–134; hereafter cited in the text as *HF.*

20. Brogan, *Life,* 70–71.

21. Remy de Gourmont, *A Night in the Luxembourg,* trans. Arthur Ransome (London: Steven Swift, 1912).

22. *Oscar Wilde: A Critical Study* (London: Methuen, 1912; 2d ed., 1913), vi; hereafter cited in the text as *OW.*

23. *Portraits and Speculations* (London: MacMillan, 1913), 6; hereafter cited in the text as *PS.*

Chapter Two

1. *Coots in the North and Other Stories,* edited, with introduction and notes, by Hugh Brogan (London: Jonathan Cape, 1988); hereafter cited in the text as *CN.*

2. Brogan, *Life,* 250.

3. *Aladdin and His Wonderful Lamp in Rhyme,* illus. Mackenzie (London: Nisbet, n.d. [1919]), unpaginated.

4. *The Elixir of Life* (London: Methuen, 1915), 311; hereafter cited in the text as *EL.*

5. Brogan, *Life,* 101, 102.

6. *Old Peter's Russian Tales* (London: Nelson, 1916; Penguin [Puffin], 1974), 9; hereafter cited in the text as *OP.*

7. Marcus Crouch, *Treasure Seekers,* 33–34.

8. *The War of the Birds and the Beasts,* ed. Hugh Brogan (London: Jonathan Cape, 1984).

9. Margery Fisher, *Classics for Children and Young People* (South Woodchester: Thimble Press, 1986), 26.

10. *Old Peter's Russian Tales,* illus. Dmitri Mitrokhin (London: Nelson, 1938), prefatory page.
11. *The Truth about Russia* (New York: New Republic, 1918).
12. Brogan, *Life,* 237, 238, 240.
13. *Six Weeks in Russia in 1919* (London: George Allen and Unwin, 1919), vi, viii; hereafter cited in the text as *SWR.*
14. Jonathan Swift, *Gulliver's Travels* (1726; Harmondsworth: Penguin, 1967), 328, 329.
15. *The Crisis in Russia* (London: George Allen and Unwin, 1921).
16. Brogan, *Life,* 270.
17. *Racundra's First Cruise* (London: George Allen and Unwin, 1923; Rupert Hart-Davis ["The Mariners Library"], 1958), 13; hereafter cited in the text as *RFC.*
18. *The Picts and the Martyrs* (London: Jonathan Cape, 1943), 20–21; hereafter cited in the text as *PM.*
19. *We Didn't Mean to Go to Sea* (London: Jonathan Cape, 1937), 198, 200, 204; hereafter cited in the text as *WDM.*
20. Quoted in Brogan, *Life,* 294.
21. Quoted in "The Adventures of Arthur Ransome," a BBC Radio production, written by Iain Trewyn and produced by John Knight, 1986.

Chapter Three

1. Brogan, *Life,* 305.
2. *The Chinese Puzzle* (London: George Allen and Unwin, 1927), 63; hereafter cited in the text as *CP.*
3. Brogan, *Life,* 307.
4. *Mainly about Fishing* (London: A. and C. Black, 1959), 136; hereafter cited in the text as *MF.*
5. *Rod and Line* (London: Jonathan Cape, 1929; Oxford University Press, 1980), 119–120; hereafter cited in the text as *RL.*
6. Both are reprinted in *Coots in the North,* 80–102.
7. Eleanor Graham, "The Bumpus Years," *Signal* 9 (September 1972): 107.
8. Crouch, *Treasure Seekers,* 71.
9. Louis Wulff in *The Daily Mail Ideal Home Book, 1949–50,* 237; quoted by Shelley, *Arthur Ransome,* 15.
10. Shelley, *Arthur Ransome,* 11.
11. Brogan, *Life,* 409.
12. Ibid., 412.
13. *Fishing* (London: National Book League/Cambridge University Press, 1955), 14.
14. *Coots in the North,* 51–60.
15. Christina Hardyment, *Arthur Ransome and Captain Flint's Trunk* (London: Jonathan Cape, 1984), 220.
16. Brogan, *Life,* 25.
17. Ibid., 428.

Chapter Four

1. Hardyment, *Captain Flint's Trunk,* 22.
2. Ibid., 148–61.
3. Brogan, *Life,* 305.
4. *Secret Water* (1939; London: Jonathan Cape, 1947), 17; hereafter cited in the text as *SW.*
5. Hardyment, *Captain Flint's Trunk,* 197.
6. Brogan, *Life,* 384–91.

Chapter Five

1. Aidan Chambers, "The Reader in the Book," in *Booktalk* (London: Bodley Head, 1985), 41.
2. "A Contemporary Classic," *Times Literary Supplement* (Children's Book Supplement, vi), 16 June 1950.
3. *Swallowdale* (London: Jonathan Cape, 1931), 55; hereafter cited in the text as *S.*
4. *The Big Six* (London: Jonathan Cape, 1940), 392; hereafter cited in the text as *BS.*
5. Michelle Landsberg, *The World of Children's Books.* (London and New York: Simon and Schuster, 1988), 122, 123.
6. Geoffrey Trease, *Tales Out of School,* 2d ed. (London: Heinemann Educational, 1964), 140.
7. Nicholas Tucker, *The Child and the Book* (Cambridge: Cambridge University Press, 1981), 53.
8. Inglis, *Promise of Happiness,* 136.
9. Brogan, *Life,* 334–35.
10. For a fuller exploration of this see Peter Hunt, "Ransome Revisited: A Structural and Developmental Approach," *Children's Literature in Education,* 12:1 (1981), 24–33.
11. Tucker, *The Child and the Book,* 215.
12. John Rowe Townsend, *Written for Children* (Harmondsworth: Penguin [Pelican], 2d rev. ed., 1983), 185.
13. Juliet Dusinberre, *Alice to the Lighthouse* (London: Macmillan Press, 1987), 90.
14. Marcus Crouch, *The Nesbit Tradition: The Children's Novel, 1945–1970* (London: Ernest Benn, 1972), 18.
15. Inglis, *The Promise of Happiness,* 66.
16. *Coot Club* (London: Jonathan Cape, 1934), 147; hereafter cited in the text as *CC.*
17. Joan Aiken, "Purely for Love," in *Children's Literature: Views and Reviews* (New York: Scott Foresman, 1973), 151.

18. Margery Fisher, *Who's Who in Children's Books*. (London: Weidenfeld and Nicolson, 1975), 159, 160.

19. Fisher, *Classics for Children*, 61–62.

20. Bob Dixon, *Catching Them Young 1: Sex, Race and Class in Children's Fiction* (London: Pluto Press, 1977), 58.

21. Eve Garnett, *The Family from One End Street* (London: Heinemann, 1937).

22. Inglis, *Promise of Happiness,* 66–67.

23. Richard Jefferies, *Bevis,* ed. Peter Hunt, The World's Classics series (London: Oxford University Press, 1989), 236.

24. For more information, see, for example, Martin Green, *Dreams of Adventure, Deeds of Empire* (London: Routledge and Kegan Paul, 1980).

25. T. M. Longstreth, review of *Swallows and Amazons, Saturday Review of Literature,* 9 May 1931.

26. Trease, *Tales Out of School,* 139.

27. Brogan, *Life,* 2–3; A, 26–31.

28. William Wordsworth, *The Prelude,* "1805" version, Book 13, 11. 47–50.

29. *Winter Holiday* (London: Jonathan Cape, 1933), 29; hereafter cited in the text as *WH.*

30. Crouch and Ellis, *Chosen for Children.* 3.

31. *Pigeon Post* (London: Jonathan Cape, 1936), 170; hereafter cited in the text as *PP.*

32. Brogan, *Life,* 291.

33. Fisher, *Who's Who.* 352.

34. Roger Lancelyn Green, *Authors and Places* (London: Batsford, 1963), 44.31.

35. J. A. Smith, review of *The Picts and the Martyrs, Spectator,* 9 July 1943.

Chapter Six

1. Brogan, *Life,* 335–37.

2. Hardyment, *Captain Flint's Trunk,* 142–44.

3. Rudyard Kipling, "Mowgli's Brothers," in *The Jungle Book* (1894, London: Oxford University Press, 1987).

4. Henry Fielding, *Tom Jones* (1749; New York: New American Library, 1963), 65.

5. Hardyment, *Captain Flint's Trunk,* 127.

6. Ibid., 145.

7. Rosamond Lehmann, review of *The Big Six, New Statesman and Nation,* 7 December 1940.

8. Brogan, *Life,* 379.

Chapter Seven

1. Quoted by Brogan, *Life,* 345–46.
2. Amabel Williams-Ellis, review of *We Didn't Mean to Go to Sea, Manchester Guardian* (supplement), 3 December 1937, xi.
3. Kit Pearson, "Arthur Ransome," in Jane Bingham, ed., *Writers for Children* (New York: Charles Scribner's Sons, 1988), 459.
4. Inglis, *Promise of Happiness,* 141–42.
5. Quoted by Brogan, *Life,* 349.
6. Inglis, *Promise of Happiness,* 140.
7. Brogan, *Life,* 357–58.
8. Trease, *Tales Out of School,* 128.
9. Margery Fisher, *The Bright Face of Danger* (London: Hodder and Stoughton), 289.
10. Fisher, *Who's Who,* 159–60.
11. Ibid., 33.
12. Brogan, *Life,* 357.
13. "A Contemporary Classic," *Times Literary Supplement* (Children's Book Supplement, vi), 16 June 1950.
14. Cf. *Peter Duck* (London: Jonathan Cape, 1932), 159–60; hereafter cited in the text as *PD.*
15. Hardyment, *Captain Flint's Trunk,* 25, 190.
16. Brogan, *Life,* 367.
17. Wallace Hildick, *Children and Fiction* (London: Evans Brothers, 1970), 50.
18. Fisher, *Bright Face of Danger,* 289, 290.
19. Hardyment, *Captain Flint's Trunk,* 184–90.
20. Fisher, *Who's Who,* 54.

Chapter Eight

1. Pearson, *Writers for Children,* 459.
2. Trease, *Tales Out of School,* 139.
3. Ruth Nadelman Lynn, *Fantasy for Children* (New York: R. R. Bowker, 1983), 1.
4. Hardyment, *Captain Flint's Trunk,* 170.
5. Pearson, *Writers for Children.*
6. Susan Cooper, *Over Sea, under Stone* (London: Jonathan Cape, 1965), and its successors.
7. Brogan, *Life,* 329.
8. Hardyment, *Captain Flint's Trunk,* 148–61.
9. Ibid., 164–68.
10. Cf. *PD,* 223, and Robert Louis Stevenson, *Treasure Island,* chapters 12 and 13 (1883; London: Cassell, 1916), 94, 102, 103.
11. Robert Louis Stevenson, "My First Book: Treasure Island," in

Lance Salway, ed., *A Peculiar Gift: Nineteenth Century Writings on Books for Children* (London: Kestrel, 1976), 418.

12. Green, *Dreams of Adventure*, 21.

13. *Missee Lee* (London: Jonathan Cape, 1941), 334–335; hereafter cited in the text as *ML*.

14. Hardyment, *Captain Flint's Trunk*, 179.

15. Inglis, *Promise of Happiness*, 140.

16. Brogan, *Life*, 381, 379–81.

17. Ibid., 410.

18. Hardyment, *Captain Flint's Trunk*, 200–6.

19. Brogan, *Life*, 398.

20. *Great Northern?* (London: Jonathan Cape, 1947), 179. Hereafter cited in the text as *GN*.

21. "A Contemporary Classic," vi.

Chapter Nine

1. Geoffrey Trease, "The Revolution in Children's Literature," in Edward Blishen, ed., *The Thorny Paradise*, (Harmondsworth: Kestrel, 1975), 16.

2. Brogan, *Life*, 35.

3. Gillian Avery, *Childhood's Pattern* (London: Hodder and Stoughton, 1975), 221.

4. Brogan, *Life*, 419.

5. Robert Leeson, *Reading and Righting* (London: Collins, 1985), 104.

6. Roger Lancelyn Green, "The Golden Age of Children's Literature" (*Essays and Studies, 1965*), reprinted in Peter Hunt, ed., *Critical Approaches to Children's Literature* (London: Routledge, 1990), 46.

7. See George Orwell, "Boys' Weeklies," *Horizon* 1, no. 3 (1940): 174–200.

8. Mary Cadogan and Patricia Craig, *You're a Brick, Angela* (London: Victor Gollancz, 1986), 179.

9. Quoted by Leeson, *Reading and Righting*, 110.

10. Graham, "Bumpus Years," 105.

11. Crouch, *Treasure Seekers*, 38.

12. Trease, "Revolution," 14.

13. Brogan, *Life*, 305.

14. Hugh Crago, "Faintly from Elfland," *Children's Literature Association Quarterly* 13:3 (Fall 1988): 146.

15. Crouch, *Treasure Seekers*, 57.

16. Ibid.

17. Roger Lancelyn Green, *Tellers of Tales*, 4th ed. (London: Edmund Ward, 1965), 262.

18. Landsberg, *World*, 125.

19. Margaret and Michael Rustin, *Narratives of Love and Loss* (London: Verso, 1987), 60.

20. Inglis, *Promise and Happiness*, 127.

21. Humphrey Carpenter and Mari Pritchard, eds., *The Oxford Companion to Children's Literature* (London: Oxford University Press, 1984), 443.

22. M. E. Atkinson, *August Adventure* (London: Bodley Head, 1936).

23. Introduction to Katharine Hull and Pamela Whitlock, *The Far-Distant Oxus* (London: Jonathan Cape, 1937), 10; hereafter cited in the text as *FD*. (Quotations are from the ninth impression, 1945; there were, remarkably, three impressions during the war.)

24. Sheila G. Ray, *The Blyton Phenomenon* (London: André Deutsch, 1982), 152.

25. Marjorie Lloyd, *Fell Farm Holiday* (1951), *Fell Farm Campers* (1960) (Harmondsworth: Penguin).

26. Geoffrey Trease, *No Boats on Bannermere* (London: Heinemann, 1949).

27. Trease, "Revolution," 22.

28. Peter Dawlish, *Dauntless Takes Recruits* (London: Oxford University Press, 1950), 236.

29. Aubrey de Selincourt, *Family Afloat* (1940), *One More Summer* (1944) (London: George Routledge).

30. Elisabeth Mace, *Ransome Revisited* (London: André Deutsch, 1975), 42.

31. Crouch, *Treasure Seekers*, 72.

32. Mary Treadgold, *We Couldn't Leave Dinah* (London: Jonathan Cape, 1941), 88. Also noted by Fisher, *Bright Face of Danger*, 287.

33. *Spectator*, 6 December 1940, 616.

34. *Times Literary Supplement*, 13 December 1934, 894.

35. *Books*, 5 April 1942, 8.

36. Fisher, *Bright Face of Danger*, 287.

37. Landsberg, *World*, 124.

38. "*Swallows and Amazons:* How It Came To Be Written," *Horn Book*, 1930, 41.

39. *Young Wings*, 18.

40. "On Isaac Walton," *Listener*, 7 May 1953, 756–57.

Selected Bibliography

Primary Works

Children's Books

Swallows and Amazons. London: Jonathan Cape, 1930; new illustrated ed., 1931; rev. ed., 1938; Philadelphia: Lippincott, 1931; Harmondsworth: Penguin, 1962; Salem, N.H.: Merrimack, 1981.

Swallowdale. London: Jonathan Cape, 1931; Lippincott, 1932; Penguin, 1968; Merrimack, 1980.

Peter Duck. Cape, 1932; Lippincott, 1933; Penguin, 1968; Merrimack, 1980.

Winter Holiday. Cape, 1933; Lippincott, 1934; Penguin, 1968; Merrimack, 1980.

Coot Club. Cape, 1934; Lippincott, 1935; Penguin, 1969; Merrimack, 1980.

Pigeon Post. Cape, 1936; Lippincott, 1937; Penguin, 1969; Merrimack, 1980.

We Didn't Mean to Go to Sea. Cape, 1937; New York: Macmillan, 1938; Penguin, 1969; Boston: Gregg Press, 1981; Merrimack, 1983.

Secret Water. Cape, 1939; Macmillan, 1940; Penguin, 1969; Merrimack, 1980.

The Big Six. Cape, 1940; Macmillan, 1941; Penguin, 1970; Merrimack, 1980.

Missee Lee. Cape, 1941; Macmillan, 1943; Penguin, 1971; Merrimack, 1980.

The Picts and the Martyrs. Cape, 1943; Macmillan, 1943; Penguin, 1971; 1980.

Great Northern?. Cape, 1947; Macmillan, 1948; Penguin, 1971; Merrimack, 1980.

Old Peter's Russian Tales. London: Nelson, 1916; 1938 (illustrated by Dmitri Mitrokhin); New York: Stokes, 1917; Penguin 1974; Merrimack, 1984.

The Fool of the World and the Flying Ship [from *Old Peter*]. Illustrated by Uri Shulevitz. New York: Farrar, Strauss, 1968.

Aladdin and His Wonderful Lamp in Rhyme. Illustrated by Mackenzie. London: Nisbet, n.d. [1919].

The Soldier and Death. London: J. G. Wilson, 1920.

The War of the Birds and the Beasts. Edited with an introduction by Hugh Brogan. London: Cape, 1984.

Coots in the North and Other Stories. Edited with an introduction and notes by Hugh Brogan. London: Cape, 1988.

Criticism

A History of Storytelling. London: T. C. and E. C. Jack, 1909.
Edgar Allan Poe: A Critical Study. London: Martin Secker, 1910.
Oscar Wilde: A Critical Study. London: Methuen, 1912; 2d ed., 1913.
Portraits and Speculations. London: Macmillan, 1913.

Adult Fiction and Miscellaneous

The Souls of the Streets and Other Little Papers. London: Brown, Langham, 1904.
The Stone Lady: Ten Little Papers and Two Mad Stories. London: Brown, Langham, 1905.
Bohemia in London. Illustrated by Fred Taylor. London: Chapman and Hall, 1907; Oxford University Press, 1984.
The Book of Friendship: Essays, Poems, Maxims, and Prose Passages. London: T. C. and E. C. Jack, n.d. [1909].
The Book of Love: Essays, Poems, Maxims, and Prose Passages. London: T. C. and E. C. Jack, 1911.
The Hoofmarks of the Faun. London: Martin Secker, 1911.
The Elixir of Life. London: Methuen, 1915.

Fishing and Sailing Books

Racundra's First Cruise. London: Allen and Unwin, 1923; Hart-Davis, 1958.
Rod and Line. London: Jonathan Cape, 1929; Oxford University Press, 1980.
Fishing. Readers' Guides, 2d series. London: National Book League, Cambridge University Press, 1955.
Mainly about Fishing. London: A. and C. Black, 1959.

Political Writings

The Truth about Russia. New York: New Republic, 1918.
Six Weeks in Russia in 1919. London: George Allen and Unwin, 1919.
'Lenin in 1919,' in *Lenin, The Man and His Work,* by Albert Rhys Williams. New York: Scott and Seltzer, 1919. 167–87.
The Crisis in Russia. London: George Allen and Unwin, 1921.
The Chinese Puzzle. London: George Allen and Unwin, 1927.

Other

"Arthur Ransome." *Young Wings,* Junior Literary Guild, September 1935.
The Autobiography of Arthur Ransome. Edited by Rupert Hart-Davis. London: Jonathan Cape, 1976.
"A Hundred Years of Children's Books" (review of Lancelyn Green's *Tellers of Tales*). *Spectator,* 14 December 1953.
Introduction to *The Far-Distant Oxus* by Katharine Hull and Pamela Whitlock. London: Jonathan Cape, 1937.
"Isaac Walton." *Listener,* 7 May 1953, 756–57.
"A Letter to the Editor." *The Junior Bookshelf* 1, no. 4 (1936). Reprinted in Marcus Crouch and Alec Ellis, eds., *Chosen for Children.* London: Library Association, 1977.
"*Swallows and Amazons:* How It Came To Be Written." *Horn Book,* May 1930, 38–44.

Translations

A Night in the Luxembourg by Rémy de Gourmont. London: Steven Swift, 1912.
A Week by Iury Libedinsky. Introduction by Arthur Ransome. London: Allen and Unwin, 1923.

Rare Books Not Consulted

The ABC of Physical Culture. London: Henry J. Drane, 1904.
A Child's Book of the Garden; Pond and Stream; Things in Season. London: Traherne, 1906.
Highway and Byways in Fairyland. London: Alston Rivers, 1907.
Radek and Ransome on Russia, Being Arthur Ransome's "Open Letter to America" with a New Preface by Karl Radek. New York: Socialist Publication Society, 1918.

Secondary Works

Biography and Background

Brogan, Hugh. *The Life of Arthur Ransome.* London: Jonathan Cape, 1984. Meticulously researched standard work.
Hardyment, Christina. *Arthur Ransome and Captain Flint's Trunk.* London: Cape, 1984. An investigation of the background of Ransome's books, showing how real landscape, incidents, people, and boats were

incorporated into the novels. Prints interesting unpublished material, and her detective work reveals hitherto unknown facts.

Wardale, Roger. *Arthur Ransome's Lakeland.* Clapham, England: Dalesman, 1988. A collection of photographs, old and new, of the real scenes of the "Swallows and Amazons" books, with a good brief introduction.

Dawson, John. "Swallows and Amazons." *Lancashire Life,* September 1978, 45–47. A brief illustrated introduction.

Criticism

Avery, Gillian. "Arthur Ransome." In *20th Century Children's Writers,* edited by D. L. Kirkpatrick, 637–38. London and Chicago: St. James Press/Macmillan, 1983.

Carpenter, Humphrey, and Mari Pritchard. *The Oxford Companion to Children's Literature.* London: Oxford University Press, 1984.

"A Contemporary Classic." *Times Literary Supplement,* 16 June 1950.

Crouch, Marcus, and Alec Ellis, eds. *Chosen for Children.* 3d ed. London: Library Association, 1977.

Fisher, Margery. *The Bright Face of Danger.* London: Hodder and Stoughton, 1986.

———. *Classics for Children and Young People.* South Woodchester: The Thimble Press, 1986.

———. *Who's Who in Children's Books.* London: Weidenfeld and Nicolson, 1975.

Haigh, Gerald. "50th Anniversary of *Swallows and Amazons.*" *Times Educational Supplement,* 14 November 1980.

Hunt, Peter. "Arthur Ransome's *Swallows and Amazons:* Escape to a Lost Paradise." In *Touchstones: Reflections on the Best in Children's Literature,* vol. 1, edited by Perry Nodelman, 221–31. West Lafayette, Ind.: Children's Literature Association, 1985.

———. "Ransome Revisited: A Structural and Developmental Approach." *Children's Literature in Education* 12, no. 1 (1981): 24–33. Suggests that as the series develops, the narrative shapes reflect a different implied audience.

Inglis, Fred. *The Promise of Happiness: Value and Meaning in Children's Fiction,* 124–45. Cambridge: Cambridge University Press, 1981. Inglis discusses Ransome in terms of class, culture, and society.

Landsberg, Michele. *The World of Children's Books.* London and New York: Simon and Schuster, 1988.

Pearson, Kit. "A Second Look: 'Swallows and Amazons.'" *Horn Book* 54, no. 5 (October 1983): 601–5.

———. "Arthur Ransome." In *Writers for Children,* edited by Jane Bingham, 459. New York: Charles Scribner's Sons, 1988.

Rota, Anthony. "Some Uncollected Authors. *The Book Collector* 8 (1959): 289–93.

Shelley, Hugh. *Arthur Ransome.* A Bodley Head Monograph. London: The Bodley Head, 1960; New York: Walck, 1964. An enthusiastic "appreciation," with little criticism of any interest.
Townsend, John Rowe. *Written for Children.* 2d rev. ed. Harmondsworth: Penguin (Pelican), 1983.

Index

The Author

Peter Hunt received his B.A., M.A., and Ph.D. from the University of Wales, and is senior lecturer in English and Children's Literature at the University of Wales College of Cardiff. He is the author of *Criticism, Theory, and Children's Literature* (1990) and has written widely on criticism and children's literature. He edited Richard Jefferies's *Bevis* and the essay collection *Children's Literature: The Development of Criticism*. He has written six children's and young adult books, which include 1989's *Sue and the Honey Machine* and *Going Up*. He is currently working on a sequel to *Going Up* and travels widely as a consultant on technical communication.